Issues in Indian History, Politics and Society
(Select Newspaper Articles and Book Reviews)

ISSUES IN INDIAN HISTORY, POLITICS AND SOCIETY

(Select Newspaper Articles and Book Reviews)

Harbans Mukhia

AAKAR

Issues in Indian History, Politics and Society
Harbans Mukhia

First Published, 2009
Reprinted, 2020, 2026

ISBN 978-93-5002-010-4

Published by
AAKAR BOOKS
28 E Pocket IV, Mayur Vihar Phase I
Delhi 110 091 India
www.aakarbooks.com

Laser Typeset at
Arpit Printographers, Delhi

Printed at
D.K. Fine Art Press, Delhi

For
Sudeep and Sunetra,
Neelanjana and Suranjan,
my generation next.

Contents

III. Book Reviews

Preface

The pieces of writing in this anthology extend over a period of a little more than a quarter century. Some of these were written as quick reactions to events in the public sphere; others, especially ones centred on the cataclysmic Ram Janmabhumi-Babri masjid dispute of the 1980s and 90s, resulted from in-depth historical research, including a visit to the site before the masjid fell to the politics of the Sangh Parivar on 6 December 1992. The one thread that runs through the anthology is an 'aware' citizen's response to issues that concern us all.

Section I on 'Perspectives' is spread over several themes. A few of them are marked by a certain immediacy, as responses to passing events. 'The State and History' (pp. 55-57) and 'Ray of Hope in Kashmir?' (pp. 70-73) have this character. Others seek to understand more durable phenomena, such as the 'Collapse of Communism' (pp. 42-45), the changing nature of history writing, 'Let Every Truth Become Suspect' (pp. 74-76), the predilection of our political Left to attempt suicide repeatedly, 'Yesterday Once More' (pp. 77-79), or understanding the notion of feudalism (pp. 80-82). The opening piece, 'The Fantasy of Power' (pp. 11-13) attempts to explore the sociology of slogan shouting and the next, 'Middle Class Dichotomy' (pp. 14-16), the phenomenon of pervasive corruption in our middle classes and their undying yearning for a clean polity and clean economy. A couple of the writings are in response to some assaults on my academic discipline, history, from those who had become by the way 'historians', even as they traversed other roads to earn their living.

Section II is more focused on the all important issue, and the specifically Indian phenomenon, of communalism. Understandably the Babri masjid dispute recurs several times here. But it also seeks to explore the problematic of communalism in general, both in its majoritarian manifestation as well as its minority, especially Muslim, character. The first entry in this Section is a vintage 1983 piece and the last is from June 2009. Over this quarter century, the author's views have not remained frozen; they would have if he could claim monopoly of the ultimate truth. Such claims are best left to great historical figures, such as Christ, Muhammad or Marx; for a passing historian, the eternal character of his opinions would be a damning testimony to a fossilized mind.

Section III reproduces a few of the author's many book reviews; the ones here are mainly of books with a more than academic interest.

Contrary to my personal view that newspaper articles have a life of no more than 24 to 48 hours, Mr K K Saxena of Aakar Books has persisted in persuading me that interest in them lasts longer, and they deserve to be put together in a book. I have thus given in to his optimism. My gratitude to him would not diminish one bit even if he is proved wrong.

June 2009

I. Perspectives

The Fantasy of Power

The Pioneer, 26.01.1996

Slogan-shouting draws within the realm of possibility that which would normally seem beyond it

The multi-faceted nature of the sociology of slogans notwithstanding, it has yet to turn into a subject of analysis.

Primarily, slogans create a fantasy of power, which draws within the realm of the possible that which would seem to be beyond it in the normal state. A demand raised in the ordinary course might appear outrageous to those in authority, but raised as a slogan it is taken in one's stride. The very experience of the poetry of rhyming slogans and the musical rhythm of shouting them makes it an extraordinary moment, counterposed to the normal state, which is marked by prosaic conversation.

The ambience of the extraordinary moment gets considerably enhanced by the merger of individuals in a collective and in collective shouting of slogans at a much higher pitch than in normal conversation. This reinforces the fantasy of power whose magnitude far outweighs the aggregate of the voices of persons doing the shouting. It also inverts the power relations between the group and the object of its wrath and slogans—the employer, the boss, or a high representative of governmental authority.

The fantasy of power, inversion and the possibility of the impossible is graphically evoked in the most popular slogans like '*Jo humse takrayega, choor choor ho jayega*' (Whoever dares to take us on will be turned into dust), or '*Murdabad*' (death and destruction be upon you). These are usually aimed at an adversary whose own institutionalised power is immense relative to that of the slogan-shouters.

Whether or not slogan shouting is a battle with an adversary, it is always turned into a form of mobilisation for a cause that is higher than oneself—the cause of the profession, the community, the party or the country. Identifying with a collectivity is easy to project as making a personal sacrifice and ennobling oneself without incurring much expense. In January 1963, ordinary citizens, including school and college teachers of Delhi, were mobilised to shout patriotic slogans at the Republic Day Parade, following the disastrous experience on the borders with China. It did not quite persuade China to rethink strategy, but it did give the ordinary Indians a chance to establish a manifest identity with the country, at least for the hours the parade lasted.

Coining and raising slogans on behalf of political parties at election times is one of the great delights of Indian democracy. Once again, it creates a fantasy of electoral support and confidence often far in excess of the ground reality. The assumption here is that the reality would mould itself in the footsteps of the fantasy, that the loud volume of vocal support will create the impression of invincibility and would, in turn, bring about the desired victory. The same thing happens in tournaments, where collective identities are in contest.

It is this ambience of space between fantasy and reality that lends movement to the functioning of democracy. Fantasy becomes as real a force as the economy or the law and both help release tensions and give a sense of participation in the social and political processes.

But raising slogans is also an act of controlling the behaviour of one's supporters. If a procession of protesters showed any signs of restlessness and breaking imposed restraints, one of the quickest and subtlest ways of re-establishing order is to lead them into slogan shouting—its rhythm itself is an effective mode of containing chaos at the seams. It is also a means of silencing dissidence within one's ranks. If in a public meeting dissidence crosses the limits of the leaders' comfort, resort is taken to slogan-shouting and drowning the dissident voice in the resounding decibles.

Coining of slogans and organising groups of slogan shouters also provide many semi-employed or unemployed youth with part-time employment for a good number of days round the year, but especially at election time. It also gives them opportunities for expressing their creative urges, either as unrecognised poets, or as make-up artists who specialise in dressing up often the same group of persons for different roles, meticulously catering to the requirement of each situation.

Middle Class Dichotomy

The Pioneer, 25.4.1995

The dream of an honest and upright politician will never die

The Indian Middle Class consists of so many strata that it defies categorisation under a single term class, which would imply a considerable degree of homogeneity. Yet, two paradoxical features characterise its conduct fairly uniformly: Extensive practice and intensive abhorrence of corruption.

In the several recent surveys of popular perceptions of corruption, politicians of course inavariably and understandably top the list, closely followed by bureaucrats, policemen, lawyers, businessmen and business executives, etc.: the quintessential middle class. If teachers do not figure high on this priority list, it is not for lack of trying, but for lack of opportunities. Over the decades and the years, the sense of shock over acts of corruption in the middle class has witnessed a steady decline, as its ambitions for a better material life have soared but the resources for meeting such ambitions have not kept pace.

What is fascinating, however, is the intense yearning of this class for a clean, corruptionless polity and society, a yearning that has again and again surfaced with any figure, public or obscure, focusing on his mission of eradicating corruption. Even the repeated failure of this promise on virtually everyone's part has not subjected it to the law of diminishing returns. The unprecedentedly massive electoral and moral support that Rajiv Gandhi was able to generate was precisely because of his political naivete which was transmuted into the image of 'Mr. Clean' for whom Indian polity had waited so long. Instantly, he became the apple of the media's eye, whose smiles ever reflected such sweet innocence and who was forgiven many a political and verbal *faux pas* precisely as one overlooks a child's pranks. What this class, however, could not forgive him was association with corruption. Overnight the innocent child had become a stereotypical, cynical politician.

But another messiah has risen to take the society into the land of honesty, burying the demon of corruption behind: Mr. V.P. Singh. He, too, was forgiven many initial resemblances with the familiar politician next door. Mr. Singh has shortcomings, but the politician in him established standards of honesty that revived memories of Gandhi. The crash came when, to fight the fire in his own backyards, he suddenly and most unexpectedly announced reservation of jobs. Quite besides the fact that Government jobs are closely linked with the middle class aspirations in India, the urban petty bourgeoisie felt let down by the crash of that larger-than-life image which had raised him above all the petty manouevres that have come to be accepted as the hallmark of the stereotypical politician. The people seemed to have turned angry with themselves for seeing a big man in what was essentially a petty figure.

But did the dream really die? A small glimmer of hope raised its head when a petty and obscure bureaucrat, Mr. G. Khairnar, took on the mantle of challenging the corrupt politician and once again the media flashed his pictures and interviews and his name began to worm into conversations in the drawing rooms. Once again a larger-than-life picture was being created. Mr. Khairnar, however, did not have the capacity to emerge as the star figure, a true messiah who could take on the whole corrupt system. Quietly then he was dumped by the media and the drawing rooms. But the dream was constantly in search of a befitting human figure. Mr. T.N. Seshan is now that figure whose campaign for probity in public life, initially manifest in electoral probity, has begun to loom large over the public imagination. The messiah is here again and, as he admitted in a recent TV interview, he is willing!

What is the significance of this repeated revival of fantasy by those grounded in the hardest realities of life? One is that life is not made of hard realities alone but as much by fantasies. Fantasy and reality are thus not quite dichotomous, nor is fantasy automatically 'rectified' or abandoned as it stands face-to-face with harsh reality. Thus corruption, or rather anti-corruption will always remain a live and explosively emotive issue in Indian politics and not all the failures on this front will be able to eliminate the dream of a clean polity. It also demonstrates that a large space of ambiguity between the practice and hostility towards corruption within the same class continues to exist and that practice does not carry any privilege within that space. Thus to dismiss the middle class urge for probity in public life as sheer hypocrisy of a class itself steeped in corruption is taking a simplistic view of things.

Mr. V. P. Singh was the messiah as long as he focused on Bofors; but he became the villain when he turned to the issue of caste! As the great equaliser in Indian politics, corruption becomes a safe issue because it becomes a crusade against all parties and thus always meets with a dead end. But it does have the potential of a non-political solution—a messianic figure seeking a mandate on resolving the problem outside the political process, as many a general has done in several countries even though without success. He can be fairly certain of rallying this very vocal and volatile class behind!

By Writing Secular History You Can't Produce a Secular Polity

Interview

The Pioneer, 20.6.1995

About Marxism and history's relevance in society

Is there any compatibility today between the dominant economic discourse in the country and the goals of social science research (SSR)?

The economic goals and social science goals are not static but dynamic. Sometimes there is cohesion and sometimes discordance. The goal of SSR has always been that of a critic—a critical evaluation lending strength to the system. From the 1950s to the early 1980s when two alternative models of totalising conceptions of society—communist and capitalist—operated, one could visualise a much greater role of SSR as a critic. Now with the dissolution of alternatives and with the emergence of a consensual world view, that role of a critic from an alternative standpoint has declined considerably. There is now a far lower level of discordance between the emerging economic order and objectives of SSR.

In the past eminent academics were also members of political parties. Should an academic be also an activist?

I myself was a member of CPM which later I gave up. So were various other great academics like Randhir Singh and Irfan Habib. At that time we did not find any incompatibility between an academic and an activist. We enjoined upon ourselves the responsibility to be actively involved in changing society. For us it was immoral to preach change while not being actively involved. But later I realised that party discipline and academic freedom (even freedom on Marxian lines) often come into serious conflict.

Though we are sticking to Marxist ideology, we do not approve of party discipline which restricts academic freedom. As you see, the intellectual output of the erstwhile socialist countries was dismal. Creative Marxism or Marxism as an intellectual pursuit flourished in the West, not in the erswhile Soviet Union. Thus, there is a considerable degree of discordance between party discipline and academic freedom.

There are several interpretations of history—nationalist, Marxian, subaltern, etc. Why is the nationalist version only being taught in the school texts? There is a consensus in our society over the nationalist or Gandhian history. But this consensus has certain biases built into it. It is largely upper caste, Hindu and upper class bias.

When they say India is a land of composite culture or talk of tolerance, they trace it to Hindu tolerance. When one speaks of abolishing untouchability, there is already a condescending attitude towards the lower castes. Now the lower castes are gradually speaking against biases built in the nationalist history and such remarks are being heard, like Mayawati's dig at such history.

The Marxist and subaltern interpretations have influence at a high intellectual plane. You cannot write a subaltern school textbook which is extremely difficult. The Marxist one is far more difficult to explain at the school level.

Has historical research helped in ascertaining the facts about the Babri Masjid dispute?

At the level of professional history, I think it has been firmly established that no temple existed underneath the mosque. If it were a dispute among historians in a seminar, then I think it would have been fairly argued that there was no temple. As a historian I would like to study the development of popular memory about the temple. It is interesting to study how this popular mentality as an aspect of history has grown and why.

Those who forget history are condemned to repeat it. Which aspects of history have been forgotten by the people as India marches into the 21st century?

"Those who forget history..." —It is only a quip without any profundity. I do not take it as a serious kind of entry point for studying society. Greatest mistakes in history have been destructive wars. But nobody has learnt from history that wars are destructive. I think Ashoka was the only one who learnt from the Kalinga war. Further, I quote: "History never repeats itself but it is the historians who repeat themselves."

What do think of the relevance of history for the society?

History has a remote kind of relevance for the society. In the early 1960s eminent historians like Nurul Hasan, R.S. Sharma and A.R. Desai thought that communalism has grown because communal history was being taught. They changed history writing by making it secular. But by writing secular history you cannot produce a secular polity. In fact the problem of communalism has grown despite our emphasis on secular history. Writings have become irrelevant.

Polity as Theatre

How vision loses out to frenzy

Indian Express, 28.12.2000

Among other things the Ram Janambhoomi movement did was to substitute frenzy as a form of political mobilisation, in place of competing political visions based upon alternative worldviews. December 6 has come to acquire the status of a metaphor for the wild destructive energy let loose on the Babri Masjid on that fateful day, when the state led by the Congress at the Centre and the Bharatiya Janata Party in UP quietly abdicated all its responsibilities towards maintaining social order, besides protecting life and property.

During the long-drawn freedom struggle, the injection of religious element by the Muslim League earned it universal disapproval, except from its own followers. In the first decade after Independence, the competing strategies of development, whether left or right, 'progressive' or 'reactionary', as they were labelled then, were furiously debated and advocated, with the middle path thrown in as Nehru's option. To back these strategies there were of course massive demonstrations and public discourses, strikes and state repression. But frenzy was not a part of these actions.

Frenzy was first experimented with by BJP's predecessor, the Bharatiya Janta Sangh and its most able orator, Atal Behari Vajpayee, as the dispute between Indian and China over land in the North-East in the late 1950s, culminating in the war of November 1962, when Nehru described the barren land in that region in a graphic phrase — 'not a blade of grass grows'

—and prepared for some sort of negotiated settlement, Vajpayee put his oratorical skills to maximum use to stop any kind of negotiation involving transfer of "even an inch of the sacred motherland". Nehru paid put in his efforts. Chester Bowles, the US ambassador put it vividly, 'Diplomacy lost out to democracy'.

This new element of frenzy was retrieved in the course of the Ayodhya dispute in the late 1980s and early 1990s and forced upon the political scenario by the BJP under the leadership of L.K. Advani and M.M. Joshi,besides the lower rung of the more vituperative leaders such as Sadhavi Rithambhra and Uma Bharati. Things began to change drastically.

History elswhere has witnessed frenzy as a mode of mobilisation on a vast scale. Muhammad himself had done wonders for his religion with frenzy as a strong driving force and his followers carried on with his legacy, though, to be sure, this was not his only lagacy. The 11th-century crusades were similarly driven by religious zeal. They constitute a major episode in the evolution of European Christian perception of Islam and the Muslim world.

Frenzy was brought to a high watermark by Adolf Hitler when he mobilised his SS volunteers on the basis of intense antipathy towards a part of the nation and a part of history, i.e. the Jews, a model that had greatly inspired M.S. Golwalkar, the second Sarsanghchalak of the RSS. On a much reduced scale, Indira Gandhi's acolytes too tried out the tactics when they used to bring in hordes of Congress 'volunteers' shouting themselves hoarse in support of some or the other minor action of hers.

The BJP thus has several historical precedents across the spectrum to fall back upon, with varying results. It must ask itself the question and the country must repeat the question to itself: Do we, in the 21st century, have the option to go along the same path that humanity has trodden in one way or another in the hoary past?

Historical evidence regarding the existence of a Ram

temple beneath the Babri Masjid is not the issue; it is one of political direction and social vision. History in any case yields precious little to support the theory of a Ram temple, or any temple, on the site of the Babri Masjid. The earliest concrete and unambiguous evidence that the site was the birthplace of Ram comes from a Persian language document, written by one Hafizullah, submitted to the Faizabad court in 1822, nearly three centuries after the construction of the mosque. As any practising historian would testify, the value of documentary evidence declines in keeping with its distance in time from the event it refers to. Thus, a document of 1822 is poor evidence for authenticating an event of 1528. Indeed, even this evidence speaks of Ram Janamasthan (the very word used in the document in Persian script) but does not speak of a temple there. There was of course considerable demolition of temples (and, incidentally, demolition of some mosques by Hindu rulers) in medieval India, but such was not the case at Ayodhya. But then, even if historical evidence were to prove conclusively that Babur had actually destroyed the temple, which would be quite contrary to his personal characteristics, are we poised in the 21st century to go back to the 16th and justify it?

The state in every medieval society looked upon itself as the site of a theatre where roles were performed according to a script for the common people to emulate. As long as theatrical roles had the desired effect, no further questions needed to be asked. Modern Indian polity still seems to follow the same script: Some dramatic action on the part of one or another segment of the political class and the people will back it. Demolish the Babri Masjid; explode a bomb, do not allow Parliament to function, announce that the Babri Masjid fell to a bomb rather than to the hammers of those atop the domes and frenzy of those behind the microphones, and you have the masses voting for you.

People themselves engage in some sort of drama by exploding crackers and doing bhangra, but when it comes to political choice, they have again and again shown their yearning for clean, development-oriented politics. Anyone exhibiting the slightest promise of cleaning up politics becomes the darling of the masses. Remember the popularity of the early Rajiv Gandhi, V.P. Singh, T.N. Seshan, and others who had the image of a crusader for clean politics.

The question then that stares us all in the face is: Have we matured as a nation to sit back and discuss and decide our destiny, or, are we yet to allow frenzy to guide us into the middle ages? We do expect our political class to reconsider its strategy of polity as theatre, where the basic assumption is that the masses are a pack of fools with no mind of their own; and we do expect Vajpayee to give us a shade better governance than his poetry.

Understanding Terrorism

TOI, 24.7.2006

A response to failings of liberal democracy

One of the surprises to emerge from recent terrorist acts around the world is the involvement of highly successful elite professionals who kill themselves even as they take numerous other lives. The Al-Qaida operatives who perpetrated 9/11 in the US were after all trained pilots flying some of the most advanced jets; some others are known to be software professionals. The Mumbai train explosions seem to carry a similar stamp.

The surprise arises from the easy assumption that terrorists' desperation is a manifestation of their community's poverty and the remedy lies in improving its economic lot. Clearly, the facts and the assumption do not cohere. We need perhaps to look for something beyond unemployment and poverty, for a much larger picture for an explanation. Does it possibly lie in the conflict between the ambitions of liberal democracy and anterior forms of democratic assertions?

There are two basic premises of liberal democracy—liberty and equality. The social unit of account is the individual. When the French Revolution proclaimed liberty, fraternity and equality as its goal, the reverberations of the three evocative words were felt around the world. The individual must be liberated from all forms of social control, those of the family, community, church or state. Its assumption was the inevitable universal triumph of the values embedded in liberal democracy and its driving force was the force of reason, in opposition to all anterior forms of thought, primarily religion.

Nineteenth century positivism reinforced the objectivity and finality of liberal democracy's universalist assumption. It thus locked itself in adversity with the earlier historically evolved forms; it virtually sought to advance by entering into a head-on clash with history.

Through history the urge for equality has asserted itself in different modes in various regions of the world; implicit in this urge was also the search for liberation. Several religious expressions, especially those centred on a monotheistic imaging of God, such as Christianity, Islam and Sikhism, have been instrumental in major social upheavals primarily moved by their egalitarian appeal. Marxism has seen the most recent secular upheaval with the same appeal.

If liberal democracy privileges the individual in its search for equality, all the others seek the same goal by subordinating the individual's aspirations to the aspirations of the community (or in the case of Marxism to the party) of which they are members. Clearly then there have been diverse manifestations of the urge for equality, and liberal democracy has the briefest history behind it with the exception of Marxism. However, in its quest for universal triumph it seeks to establish uniformity over the diverse landscape of history. It enters into an almost irresoluble conflict with all anterior forms of the search for egalitarianism.

The chief operative instrument in the realisation of democracy is the holding of periodic elections. Universal adult franchise, itself with no more than six or seven decades of history behind it in the most advanced democracies of the West, is the medium of ensuring equality to all its citizens. However, incapable as the instrument is of establishing a decisive democratic superiority of a majority vote of, say, 51 per cent over a rival vote of 49 per cent, the history of electoral democracies almost around the world has in any case witnessed the rule of governments elected by a minority vote. What then would be the measure of democratic legitimacy of such regimes which are the rule than the exception?

Liberal democracy also functions through an integral link with the market and capitalism. The supremacy of the market as the great equaliser at work here would be hard to sustain in the context of history which has witnessed the market as the instrument of differentiation and hegemonisation within societies and between them. It was the driving force of imperialism and colonialism for nearly two centuries before the Second World War. The state has intervened and decisively removed obstacles to market expansion within a nation and globally. Under liberal democracy's auspices it yet forms the sole premise for the attainment of freedom and equality around the world.

The finality of this one vision of equality and liberty, with the assumption of its inevitable universal triumph over the others, needs to be critically scrutinised and space for plurality of vision and their mutual tolerance be enlarged exponentialy where historical and cultural experiences of all segments of humanity become part of the process of a shared but diversified human future.

We also need to evolve a large range of institutional forms for realising democratic aspirations, with electoral democracy being just one of them. The material comforts of life that the vote and the market provide to those successful ones in a competitive ambience are clearly not a compensation enough for the loss of historical and cultural legacies.

Reflections of the past

Indian Express, 30.4.1989

Professor Harbans Mukhia replies to the critique of the Marxist interpretation of medieval Indian history

Sita Ram Goel's 'examination' of what he insists is the Marxist interpretation of medieval Indian history ('Some historical questions', *Indian Express*, April 16) is based upon the following assumptions:

1. All historians who have any doubt whatsoever about religious bigotry being the sole driving force of the medieval Indian state are Marxists;

2. All Marxist historians follow a given Party line and in the process suppress, distort or explain away facts; they also manoeuvre themselves into controlling positions of the academia which they use unscrupulously to popularise false history;

3. True history, therefore, must be rescued from their clutches; and true history is nothing if not the assertion that the Muslim rulers of medieval India, motivated by 'a full-fledged theology which inspired Islamic iconoclasm', were spending their time demolishing Hindu temples and, one supposes, converting the Hindus to Islam or else putting them to the sword (though Mr. Goel has failed specifically, if perhaps forgetfully, to make this point); and finally,

4. Any evidence that the demolition of places of worship of different denominations was not the monopoly of Muslim rulers is, of course, 'of doubtful veracity'.

Heroic as Mr. Goel's attempt to rescue the truth from the

hands of the baddies is, his familiarity with medieval Indian history, and with the historiography of the past quarter century, has not quite kept pace with his brave intention; and in this era of *glasnost* the world over, it is quaint that all Mr. Goel can see is flaming red in every historian who does not abide by his single version of the truth!

The historiography of medieval India from the 1920s onwards was indeed conditioned by a central concern: the Hindu–Muslim relations during those medieval centuries. The concern was a projection backwards of the chief issue of the freedom struggle itself, nemely communalism, in both its Congress and the Muslim League or the Hindu Mahasabha versions. What divided the two was a very thin line: the Congress nationalism emphasised 'Hindu–Muslims *bhai-bhai* ethos and the League–Mahasabha communalism treated Hindus and Muslims as enemies—but both had religious denomination as their central analytical category.

These visions were the ones reflected backwards into medieval Indian history: the 'Hindu–Muslim *bhai-bhai*' syndrome at the hands of nationalist historians such as Mohammad Habib, Tara Chand, R.P. Tripathi, B.P. Saxena, etc. and the communalist one at those of R.C. Majumdar, I.H. Qureshi and so forth. If one set of historians highlighted evidence of communal co-existence and harmony in medieval centuries, often by ignoring contrary evidence, the other overstated acts of communal tensions, also ignoring contrary evidence. Incidentally, the sources of evidence for both were the same, namely, court chronicles written in the Persian language.

The post-Independence generation of historians had other preoccupations than one of obsession with religion; thus a multi-faceted, rather than a monocausal, study of history began to develop. This generation was willing to accord religion its due place in historical explanation, but no monopoly. It was also realised that if contrary evidence existed regarding religious policies of the same rulers, clearly the explanation must lie outside of merely the personal beliefs or attitudes of those rulers. These historians examined the religious policy of the state, not as an independent variable, but as part of the totality of political policies. They put the entire gamut of often contrary bits of evidence together and sought to explain the paradox.

It was thus that Iqtidar Alam Khan, in a research paper, traced the evolution of Akbar's religious stance in three phases—the liberal, the orthodox and the liberal again—each in the context of his changing political compulsions. So that far from papering over the evidence of a phase in Akbar's reign when he adopted an orthodox religious posture, I.A. Khan was the first historian to have brought to light the temporary reimposition of the *jazia* by the self-same Akbar, after having abolished it earlier. I am sure Mr. Goel has not read, nor heard of this piece of research by one who is actually a committed Marxist historian. A similar approach was adopted by M. Athar Ali in his major work, *Mughal Nobility Under Aurangzeb,* published in 1966, where be put together evidence and placed emphasis on Aurangzeb's large scale demolition of Hindu temples; but he also came across evidence of the extension of land and revenue grants to other Hindu temples by the same emperor. This latter evidence, Mr. Goel might be surprised to know, was not the figment of Athar Ali's imagination—it had been collected and published by K.K. Datta, in *Some Sanads, Firmans and Parwanas (1578-1802)*, in 1962 and later on by B.N. Goswami and J.S. Grewal in *The Mughals and the Jogis of Jakhbar*, 1967. And a great many similar documents wait in various archives, including the National Archives, to be put together and published.

Mr. Goel might have noticed that none of these last three historians is a Muslim, whose word would *ipso facto* be 'of doubtful veracity' for him; and, as a committed Marxist historian myself, let me assure Mr. Goel that none of them is a Marxist though each is an outstanding historian without whose contribution our understanding of the medieval past would have been much the poorer. Using these bits of evidence, Athar Ali too traced phases, in place of the earlier assumed uniformity, in the evolution of Aurangzeb's religious policy, again seeking explanation for it as part of the evolving political policies of his reign. By ordering the demolition of temples on one hand and simultaneously giving grants to them on the other, Aurangzeb was clearly seeking the support of orthodox Sunni Muslim and orthodox Hindu sections of the nobility at the same time when he was faced with a crisis. Indeed, need we be surprised by such management of politics after being witness to Rajiv Gandhi's pandering to conservative Muslim leadership, by passing the Muslim Women's Bill, and to conservative Hindu sentiment by having the locks on the Ram Janambhoomi opened, both done at nearly the same time?

It is in this same context, of treating religion as a political resource, like other resources, with which rulers everywhere and at all times operate, that the incidents of even Hindu rulers, like King Harsha, demolishing Hindu temples, and desecrating Buddhist and Jaina places of worship, have been cited by several historians. Mr. Goel of course would not believe that this could be true; at best, such incidents would be marginal, of no significance, compared to the central thrust of 'Muslim' rule in India, indeed its *raison d'etre,* the elimination of non-Islamic religions. Who is explaining away inconvenient facts, Mr. Goel?

Historical truth, like other truths, is much more complex and varied than Mr. Goel's virginal simplicity of faith seems to assume. Historical research has been enormously enriched by the recent contributions of a very large number of historians, of a whole spectrum of colours and hues; and this enrichment has come with the realisation that its driving force is academic disputation even amongst historians of the same school. Mr. Goel can revel in the certitude of his knowledge which stopped growing at least 25 years ago and make wild allegations out of sheer ignorance, but knowledge, perhaps much to his chagrin, has not stopped growing!

There is No Need to Walk Away from CPM's Dilemmas

TOI, 10.8.1990

Mr. Praful Bidwai is not the first to characterise the CPM as a Stalinist party, nor, undoubtedly, would he be the last. In doing so, however, he is making just about half the point, in itself quite valid; the other half is that the CPM is practically the first Stalinist party which adapted itself to a multi-party parliamentary democracy even though it is itself not quite used to internal democratic functioning. The significance of this fact becomes clearer if we recollect that other Stalinist communist parties operating in parliamentary politics have either been marginalised or crushed with a heavy hand. If the CPM has survived either of these fates, it is because it accepted the rules of parliamentary democracy even as it denounced the same democracy as a bourgeois phenomenon. It has also demonstrated that however desirable intra-party democracy might be, it is no necessary prerequisite for full participation in the democratic system outside. Indeed, the CPM is not the only party to have done so; the Congress too has set a record of sorts along these lines.

The problem, however, lies somewhere else. Even as the communist movement has denounced parliamentary democracy as bourgeois (not without reason), it has failed to devise an alternative political system. In fact, often the best allies of the communist movement have been those fake democracies whose legitimacy was patently questionable. But whenever face-to-face with a functioning parliamentary democracy, it has always found itself in a no-win situation.

Moreover because of the credibility that the democratic system generally acquires, one is not left even with the option of functioning outside its framework. The only option then open is to operate within the system and thereby seek to demonstrate its limitations and its essential bourgeois character. This was the strategy adopted by the CPM in 1964 when it split from the CPI, unhappy at the parent body's absorption into parliamentary politics. Implicit in this strategy was the assumption that the CPM would in practice subordinate its parliamentary activity to the building up of an extra-parliamentary revolutionary organisation for the ultimate capture of state power. The CPM was soon to realise that, in actual practice, participation in parliamentary politics imposes structural limits to the prospect of building up an extra-parliamentary organisation.

For, contesting elections gradually enforces the necessity of winning them. Winning elections becomes a measure of popular acceptance of one's ideological and political positions. As an idealist gesture a communist party can contest elections in order to place its point of view before the people without caring for electoral victory. But it soon becomes a farcical situation when one contests an election but simultaneously has to inform the electorate of one's unconcern about it. On the other hand, gradually, the number of votes fetched by the party becomes the measure by which to judge whether or not people are responding to its point of view. The more election victories, the greater the measure of popular acceptance of one's political and ideological positions.

In the process two problems arise for political parties. First, elections are not won merely on the basis of any party's superior moral or political stand; a great deal of organisation, money, and factors like purely local issues and social composition of the electorate too influence election results. Because of this, political compromises begin first hesitantly, then slightly more openly to gain electoral victories for the higher cause. Second, obtaining the legislative majority in a state lands the communist party with the responsibility of forming a government and working it within the framework of the bourgeois constitution. Defending such a government in turn becomes an important part of the party's political activity and slowly becomes the dominant concern.

Thus, 'bourgeois' parliamentary elections become the source of legitimacy for the communist party as well. Parliamentary activity and related practices begin to involve the communist party slowly but surely, to the exclusion of the intended extra-parliamentary organisation and activities. It is thus that the very working of parliamentary politics overwhelms the subjective desire of the communist leadership to combine it with extra-parliamentary organisation. This happens at all levels — at the level of elections to parliament, assemblies, panchayats, trade unions or of students unions.

All this, however, would be true of societies with a fairly long tradition of generally free and fair elections. The picture is quite different where elections themselves are unfree and unfair. There the ruling classes themselves subvert the framework that could be expected to enclose and contain revolutionary activity. It is worth remembering that no communist party has ever been able to capture power in an established functioning democracy. On the other hand operating outside such a democratic framework leads to a situation where it is difficult for the communist parties to question the legitimacy of the bourgeois system and any effort to overthrow the system gets defeated, as the experience of the Naxalite movement shows.

It would therefore appear that a communist party, seriously committed to the idea of revolution but operating in a genuine bourgeois democratic framework faces an awful dilemma: either it opts out of the democratic framework and is therefore unable to destroy the latter's legitimacy, or works within that framework and gets absorbed in it as a Left parliamentary party. So far the communist movement has not found a way out in theory or in practice.

The Historical Backdrop

Building a new India

Employment News, 26 Jan. – 1 Feb., 1991

When we cast a glance around at today's India we are struck by the level of economic, technological and educational backwardness compared to the advanced countries of the West in particular. But was it always like this?

Let us look at two major features of the economy prior to the modern era in a comparative perspective: agriculture and industry. As far back as we can go in history most Indian lands have yielded two crops in a year. There is almost an unbroken chain of evidence—from Megasthenes in the 4th century B.C. to the *Arthasastra* of Kautilya down to the 14th century Moroccan traveller ibn Battuta and further on to British commentators of the end of the eighteenth century like Rev. William Tennant and Colebrooke—which attests to this fact. Unfortunately we have very little information about the seed:yield ratios for the very distant past but a 14th century account, the *Sunya Purana,* records the ratio as 1:12. The significance of this act gets into proper focus when we compare it with the west European agriculture productivity.

In Western Europe down to the tenth century A.D. anywhere between one-third and a half of the land under actual cultivation yielded nothing in any one year, for it had to be left fallow or uncultivated to allow the soil to regain its fertility. And the seed:yield ratio stood at a dismal 1:2.5 at best. By the 13th century, owing to certain technical devices developed in the meanwhile, the seed:yield ratio rose to 1:4

which is considered a remarkable achievement.

If the Indian land was so much more fertile it was because there was a constant natural as well as artificial renewal of the soil fertility. Being a tropical country where the harsh sun dried the moisture quickly, cultivation was concentrated in the river basins. Here, besides the annual floods, which brought in very fertile virgin soil from the hills, there was a daily deposit of the waste material that the rivers carry over long distances while grinding it and decomposing it to make it exellent manure. There was, in addition, the very swift formation of the humus in the field itself. In order to retain the moisture in the soil, the peasant merely scratched the surface; thus the waste deposits below the surface, reacting to the moisture and the heat of the sun quickly turned into manure. Then there was the artificial manure prepared by the peasants in their homesteads and their fields, particularly from the deposits of the large number of cattle that each maintained. We can guess the numbers of cattle from Emperor Akbar's stipulation in the 16th century that a peasant who possessed four oxen, two buffaloes and six goats for every plough was too poor to be taxed. It is in this context that we can well appreciate the significance of religious ban on cow slaughter from the later Vedic period onwards. Indeed, apart from the animal manure, a large number of techniques for the making of manures and fertilisers were developed by the early medieval centuries and we find these described in the text on agriculture, the *Krsi Parasara*.

In Western Europe on the other hand manure was the chief bottleneck in agricultural production until the coming of the chemical fertilisers in the 19th and 20th centuries. With the fertility of land so dismal, they had to spread out the seeds in the field so that vast fields were cultivated for obtaining a meagre subsistence. It has been estimated for example that until the tenth century a hundred acres were required to maintain one peasant family at a bare level of subsistence; in India on the other hand about 14 acres were so required.

In the use of agricultural implements similarly the state of Indian progress was far ahead of the West. The yoking of the plough to the ox by placing it on his neck to use the drawing power of his shoulder is known in the later Vedic period. Indeed, the yoking came very easy, for the typical Indian bull has a hump on his neck which would prevent the yoke from slipping. The European bull does not possess this hump; consequently the peasant there learnt to place the plough on the bull's neck only by the 8th century A.D. by way of strapping which did not constrict the bull's breathing as he moved forward. Prior to that the plough was tied to the horns of the ox by two strings, clearly a very inefficient way of using his draught power which lies in his shoulders. European progress in agriculture came through a series of technical devices and an increasingly complex rotation of crops which gradually reduced, and ultimately eliminated the system of the fallow from agricultural practice. India on the other hand registered considerable advance in the areas where it needed progress most, namely in the methods of irrigation. The three-stage development of the water-wheels—beginning with a pair of rims on which buckets were attached, going on to the attachment of a bucket-chain but without the gearing and finally the pindrum gearing—is by itself suggestive of considerable technological dynamism of the medieval Indian peasant. There are besides large and small tanks, even lakes and canals all dug for irrigation by the state, the village communities or individual peasants—all of these suggest that Indian agricultural technology was far from static. This is further attested by the impressive number of new crops and an even more impressive number of new varieties of old crops that were constantly being added on by the Indian peasant to his repertoire through the centuries.

Let us now turn to non-agricultural production. It is obvious that the biggest sector of non-agricultural production was textiles. In this sector virtually all of the West European nations were competing with one another to buy Indian textiles and sell them in their home markets throughout the

17th century. It was really a sellers' market in finished products. Clearly then the Indian products were technically as well as economically attractive enough to be the cause of such fierce competition among European buyers. The numerous European travellers in the 17th century repeatedly compliment Indian artisans for being able to reproduce almost any artifact with great skill. However, where India did lag quite far behind Europe was in the sphere of science. Technologically it was easy to reproduce an existing artifact; it was also possible to devise new artifacts through gradual modification of what was already in use. But science gives human beings a grasp over the basic principles of the working of nature and of matter; it thus allows human beings to conceive of and bring into existence phenomena hitherto unknown and unexperienced. It makes possible an advance that is not gradual but grows by leaps and bounds. India did not have a Newton or a Copernicus!

Thus down to about the 18th century the material basis of Indian economy, as compared to that of Europe, has nothing much to be ashamed of. So long as production of material goods was based on natural forces harnessed by manual energy, like in agriculture and crafts, India was a step ahead of the West. It is in the 18th and 19th centuries that the real break came leaving India and other countries of what is now called the third world far behind. This was when manual production began to give way to mechanised production and human energy gave way to energy harnessed from the natural sources such as steam, coal and electricity. This is what the grasp over scientific principles had made possible; this is where Indian skills were left way behind. The subsequent story is well known: The gradually advancing Western Europe colonised a great part of the rest of the world and squeezed its resources to fuel its own advance, and the price of that colonization is still being paid.

Socially and culturally, the dominant Indian ethos has been one of tolerance and assimilation throughout history. This is not to deny the resort to violence at various levels of society and for various purposes; that notwithstanding, the fact remains that the level of tolerance and assimilation in Indian society and culture has been of a much higher order than in several other societies. By 'Indian' we mean not merely Hindu ethos but all inclusive. Indeed even Islam, which being a proselytising religion, is by its nature bound to be more aggressive than a non-proselytising religion like Hinduism, has acquired a peculiarly Indian flavour which marks it out from Muslim societies elsewhere. In the Arab countries or in Iran, Islam virtually eliminated all traces of pre-Islamic religions in remarkably brief periods of time, in a matter of decades, on its arrival, and converted the people. In India, on the other hand, after five and a half centuries of Muslim rule the Muslims constituted just about 25 per cent of the population on the eve of Independence. The densest concentration of Muslims in pre-Partition India was as it is today, in four regions of the subcontinent: in Kashmir and Malabar and what are now Pakistan and Bangladesh. All these are situated at the peripheries of the subcontinent. In medieval India, they were also at the political peripheries of the Empire in that the hold of the Muslim state on these regions was at best sporadic and most of the time contested. It follows therefore that the state could not have engaged itself in converting masses of people in regions where its own presence was minimal. On the other hand in the regions which comprised the heartland of the Muslim empire for five and a half centuries, in Bihar, U.P. and Delhi the Muslims have never exceeded about 15 per cent of the total population. Clearly then the political Islam in India was far from being as aggressive as it was in the Arab countries or Iran.

At the social plane, as conversions to Islam took place, the converts took into their new religions so many of the old ceremonies and customs, etc. of their ancestors that are not to be found among any other community of Muslims in other counties. The ceremonies attending the birth of children, those of marriage (like the taking of *baraat* to the bride's residence) and some of the death ceremonies are specifice to Indian

Muslims because they are Hindu in their origin. Indeed, even the *tazia* of the Shia Muslims of India is unheard of elsewhere because it is an adaptation of the chariot festivals.

This liberal Indian ethos has been a great asset for the country and its civilization in its attempt to survive all the great vicissitudes through which it has passed. It gave to India a resilience so that no amount of adversity, not even repeated conquests by several foreign groups, could break and demolish the structure of India. This in itself is quite remarkable considering the history of so many regions of the world where foreign conquests completely redefined not only the history of those regions but also their society and culture, etc.

Yet, it is an open question whether this very resillence did not come in the way of India adapting itself to a fast changing world in the sphere of science, technology and above all concepts and ideas.The assimilative character of Indian culture also seems to have disabled our society from standing up to a challenge and meeting it head-on and from there to go forward. Let us take an example. Since 1950 India has been experimenting with an extraordinarily modern form of polity, namely partiamentary democracy based on universal adult franchise, which includes the women's right to votc, and multi-party elections. The modernity of this system can be appreciated if we recollect that French women obtained the voting right only six years before their Indian sisters did and in Canada women's vote came just ten years earlier than in India; even in the U.K. and U.S. it is in the 1930s that the women got this right and in a country like Switzerland this happened as late as 1973. As for multi-party elections the whole of Eastern Europe has experienced it for the very first time only in 1990. Therefore India has adopted the parliamentary system in its fully developed from just about the time that the most advanced Western countries did.

Yet, in its assimilative ethos India has sought to work this system with pre-modern operative units. That is, the units of mobilisation for parliamentary elections here have been by and large community, caste, regional identity, language, etc. etc. Thus the most important factor for political parties in selecting their candidates for a constituency usually is its communal or caste or regional group composition. In a way this has helped bring into the political mainstream those groups at the lower rungs of society which would have taken much longer to get integrated with it: the minorities, the poor, the opperessed. But in the process the very function of parliamentary politics has been diluted. The right to vote is a purely individual right and is based on the assumption that each individual will take his or her own decision on how to use it; it is also essentially a political right exercised for a political purpose where non-political considerations are seldom relevant; it therefore militates against group identities other than political grouping like political parties and it does not cater to non-political considerations like religions or caste, etc. But such has not been the case in India where these non-political identities have often become decisive in the functioning of the political system. Here an issue like the constrction of a temple at a particular site has led to the fall of a government and is likely to cast a decisive influence in the formation of another. We are thus witness to the tension between a very modern political process and its pre-modern units of operation brought to a head.

To blame this on the backwardness of Indian people's consciousness would be far from just. The vast majority of the Indian masses is educationally backward, but the same illiterate masses have a sense of political discrimination that is far beyond the ones with a high university degree. For, whenever these masses have been offered a choice between secular economic and political issues and those based on communal and caste identities, they have invariably and definitively responded in favour of secular choice, no matter who offered it. What can be a better proof of it than the elections of 1967, 1971, 1977 and to an extent 1980? It is not the illiterate masses of India who have failed in taking India forward; it is the educated urban elite which has failed to create those categories of thinking which would take India to the frontline of nations.

We have seen above how the humble peasant throughout India's long history responded quickly and positively to the needs of technological and economic development by devising irrigation systems and experimenting with ever newer crops; we have also seen that the humbler Indian artisan kept abreast of the rest of the world in the production of this craft. The failure to keep pace with the world's most advanced religions came when newer categories of thought, newer concepts were emerging in those regions and we in India kept managing with the older categories or at best to blend some of the newer categories with the age-old ones even when these were utterly incompatible. The long history of adjustment and absorption has helped Indian society and civilisation survive the radical challenges of wars, battles and religious conflicts. Today the challenges are of a different order altogether; these are challenges of concepts of science and nature, which can hardly be met in the old mode. In order to build a new India therefore we must build new categories of thinking. While giving a long history and an old civilisation their due, we must realise that they also become a major source of inertia for societies.

Collapse of Communism: Roots Lie in Marxism

TOI, 16.10.1991

The explanations for the collapse of socialist regimes in the Soviet Union and East Europe have ranged from the victory of good over evil to conspiracy hatched by imperialism to destabilise its chief adversary. If the former explanation is a simplistic reiteration of Cold War notions, the latter draws us away from the analysis of the internal failure of these regimes and is, therefore, no more satisfying than the other.

It is perhaps possible to argue that the collapse of the socialist regimes arose from the absence of any self-correcting mechanisms within the system. Parliamentary democracies have developed such a mechanism whereby not only do the temporal limits of each parliamentary mandate ensure its periodic renewal, modification or overthrow, but even within its formal duration, almost every day there is a process of adjustment and accommodation through the interplay of interest groups, caucuses and coteries.

Through this 'self-correction' (in the sense of adjustment), the system has, over time, acquired sensitivity to the pressures of a whole range of groups in society. It has responded to their cultural social and economic pressures sometimes by making concessions, at others through repression and often through a combination of both.

The communist parties were not unaware of the need for such a mechanism. Instead, they accepted that the notion of democratic centralism, combined with 'criticism and self-criticism' would guide the party's functioning. However, this principle remained no more than a moral precept, with no structures evolved for its implementation, and often used within the party for waging ruthless faction fights. It is the operation of this principle that gave rise to 'Stalinism', a term itself unsatisfactory in that it implies 'Stalinism' as being specific to the Soviet Union at a particular historical juncture, almost as an aberration. In fact 'Stalinism' is a universal feature characteristic of the working of all communist parties everywhere.

Party's failure

The failure of the party to develop these self-correcting mechanisms is rooted in the very departure that Marxist theory had sought to achieve. On the one hand, it sought to embody and articulate humanity's age-old egalitarian aspirations; on the other, it grounded these aspirations in the economic infrastructure, the mode of production, which lay at the base of all other identities. "Religion is a mere reflex of the real world," Marx, wrote in *Capital.*

The counterposition of the *real* world, i.e. the economy, and religion or culture in general, perceived as having no autonomous existence of its own, came to acquire a durability in Marxist thinking and practice that would have earned it encomiums, were it not responsible for the inertia that followed in its wake. When, after Marx's death, Marxism was charged with over-stating the role of the economy in social transformation at the expense of other facets of human existence, Engels grudgingly made concessions to these other facets like the state and politics. But, he asserted ". . .in the last instance" it was still the economy which determined everything else.

It is this permanent structuring of historical, or social change in the economic infrastructure through the instrumentation of class-struggle (class constructed in economic determinist terms) that gave birth to the communist party, as the 'vanguard' of the working class, and to the assumption that transformation of the infrastructure will, consequentially, transform human beings' culture and thinking. The working class in any case was to bring about the last transformation in history after which class-struggle would cease for all time.

Radical experiment

The socialist regimes did, indeed, conduct some radical experiments with the economy, negating private ownership of the means of production and substituting social ownership in its stead. However, the belief that this change in the sphere of economic production would also change the motivation, the driving force of the production system did not work out, based as it was on the assumption of the *permanent* structuring of the explanation of human behaviour. It turned out that human behaviour, especially group behaviour, is the result of constantly varying conjunctures. To reduce this constant variation to any kind of permanent structuring would be no better than teleology. Thus, the socialist regimes' economic experiments could not create an alternative culture, an alternative motivation. If anything, these regimes needed self-correction far more than the older ones, but the teleological assumption stood in their way. And since Marxism, more than any other mode of social analysis, staked its validity on praxis, ("Philosophers have so far interpreted the world; the point, however, is to change it", said Marx), it is hard to disown that stake, now that praxis has turned theory around. However, devoid of this validity, Marxism would nevertheless constitute a part of the intellectual legacy of humankind.

Visionary that Marx was, some of his vision might still be realised in spite of himself. He had visualised a 'communist' society where the means of production would have been so developed that technology would take over the jobs of economic production from human hands. It is only then that human beings would be able to actualise their innate artistic potential. To paraphrase him, in the communist society, one could be a musician in the morning, painter in the afternoon and critic after dinner, without ever becoming any of these professionally.

Marx had also predicted the demise of the very notion of private ownership of the means of production, of capitalism. Going by the way technology is changing the face of production, it may not be a mere delusion to think of a time when human beings would be freed from the drudgery of producing their subsistence and being musicians or painters without becoming those. It is then that the problem of ownership of the means of production may face a more challenging interrogation than the erstwhile socialist regimes were able to pose.

Polity Hampering Economy

TOI, 13.11.1991

The tyranny of shibboleths

A queer dichotomy between the economy and the polity, always implicit, is coming to the surface in today's India. At a time when the world was divided between hostile and mutually exclusive camps, the capitalist and the socialist, India, in the best tradition of its history and culture, sought to operate with an intermediate category of a mixed economy in which the hostility and the exclusiveness of the other two got dissolved. Its polity also accommodated and absorbed the communist parties, with neither a negligible nor overwhelming presence when elsewhere the parties had either established exclusive control over state power or were being marginalised or eliminated.

Worst results

Today, when the socialist experiment has come a cropper in the face of the untrammelled growth of free enterprise, shadows on the feasibility of the mixed economy seem to have understandably lengthened, particularly as it gave India the worst of both the worlds. It gave us neither the fast pace of technological and economic change which characterised capitalism, nor the security of minimum subsistence to all citizens ensured by socialism. It happens that at this very moment the problem of external debt has brought the Indian economy to the verge of collapse. Quick and decisive steps were, therefore, no longer a matter of policy options. And these steps in the present context, moved only in one direction—liberalisation, with or without IMF guidance.

The speed with which old operative categories, evolved and practised over nearly half a century, were abandoned without virtually any resistance at any level is a testimony to the sensitivity the Indian economy has acquired. However, it is important to realise that these categories were already being eroded by the differential performance of the two sectors of the mixed economy. This quick and smooth process comes into greater relief when compared to the problems the Soviet Union and East Europe are facing in making the transition from entirely state-controlled to market-driven economics.

Once the category of bureaucratic control as the driving force of economic growth, which has seven decades of 'failure' behind it, has been dumped and the enormous energy stored up in the older individual motivation, which has a history of four centuries of 'success', unleashed, it is possible that the Indian economy may begin to look up. For after all, there is no denying that human resources in India in terms of talent, ingenuity and skills are remarkable and that the process of growth in independent India has often had to contend with bureaucratic obstacles and depend upon the support of the state-sponsored infrastructure with all its inefficiency and corruption. And yet this process has been able to make some gains.

If a sense of immediacy and decisiveness has been discerned in the economic sector, it is matched by an equal amount of inertia in the sphere of politics and administration. Parliamentary politics in India has mostly operated with primordial categories of mobilisation: caste, community, regional and linguistic identities. The very success of mobilisation through these identities has naturally reinforced rather than eroded them. And since most parties have mobilised support through these identities, the success of some has egged others on to traverse the familiar and easy path with greater vigour. In the process, the distinction between the secular and the communal parties has become so blurred with the possible exception of the CPM. However, the managers of our polity show no signs whatsoever of abandoning these old operative categories which too have a history of almost half a century behind them.

The same inertia characterises thinking in virtually all spheres of political policy. In a milieu where the 19th century concept of the nation-state is getting rapidly outdated and being abandoned by some of the world's most powerful countries, and new economic and political units are being forged transcending the existing economic, political and territorial boundaries, our leaders across party divisions are constructing ever more scary visions of the siege mentality of our nation-state. The vision of such a strong state as India being besieged by much smaller powers on all sides is really the mirror image of the BJP's construction of the siege mentality of the Hindus.

Party consensus

But while the BJP endeavour within faces some resistance, however mild, the construction of a threat to India from hostile countries on all sides has achieved a political consensus of sorts across party lines. These are, however, precisely the countries with which India should have been trying seriously to work within the framework of SAARC which has now become something of a joke. The policy towards Pakistan has acquired a special durability. It usually consists of two elements—effusive statements after each of India's new prime ministers meeting with each of Pakistan's preceded and followed by strident and hostile allegations. There is a total absence of awareness that the world is at last giving up 19th-century categories of thought in almost every sphere of existence and moving towards altogether newer modes of thinking.

In administration, the situation is, if anything, far worse. Throughout history the single most important legitimising principle of the state has been its assumption of the responsibility for maintenance of the law and order. Other responsibilities have accrued or have been shed with the passage of time but this one has remained in place and will continue to do so in the future. However, it is in this sphere that the presence of the Indian state since Independence has been found lacking and the situation is getting out of hand with each passing day. We have a state which cannot even enforce traffic rules in the major cities, including the national capital. As experience is increasingly demonstrating, to expect redressal for crimes like murder and kidnapping has become a distant dream. Riots, at times causing thousands of deaths as in 1984 and subsequently, have become removed from both the judicial and policing processes. It would not be too much of an exaggeration to say that the administration has collapsed or is in the process of collapsing.

Work culture

Arising from and reinforcing political and administrative lethargy is an even more serious drag, namely the work culture, particularly in the public sector establishments. It is interesting to note how the same individuals who would take six months to write a three-line response to a legitimate query or claim in a government office, crackle with energy when managing their own enterprises outside of office hours or when they function in a different work culture as NRIs. It is easy to import computers and impart training in their use; it is far harder to realise that the computer is not merely a better typewriter and that it requires a different attitude towards work.

It is, therefore, a paradox that even as the Indian economy is perhaps poised for a leap after more than four decades of relative sloth because our leaders were forced to dump shibboleths, the political and administrative regimes merrily continue with their own shibboleths. It is clear that the inefficiency, corruption and tension resulting from these have not stirred any one in politics and administration to think afresh and ahead. It should also be evident that the economy, policy and administration do not move in autonomous circuits and that the failings of any one will slow down the economic process. The old all-absorbing ethos had the merit of easing tensions and letting Indian society survive through history when the pace of change was slow and gradual. Today, when the world is fast becoming unrecognisable, and one has to keep running even to stay in the same place, the unwillingness to abandon well-tried shibbleths can only leave us far behind even in spheres where new measures have been initiated.

Backwardness of Our Political Elite

TOI, 19.12.1991

In an interesting paradox, the working of a very modern political process in India, the parliamentary democracy, is largely based upon the mobilisation of support through primordial communal and caste identities. We have had universal adult franchise since 1950 and multi-party elections for the last 40 years.

Yet, more often than not this modern political process has been worked here with pre-modern operative units, namely caste, by most political parties. Each party seeks to corner for itself the electoral support of a combination of community and caste groups expressively captured in the term vote-bank. The BJP's endeavour of monopolising the largest vote-bank, namely the Hindus, conforms to, instead of questioning the politics of other parties.

Radical departure

The assumption made by liberal political leaders like Nehru seems to have been that given the technological, economic and educational backwardness of the Indian masses after Independence, a radical departure from the age-old identities and solidarities might be counter-productive. However, a dose of modernisation, through parliamentary democracy and rapid industrialisation, might build the bases for breaking the hold of all-round backwardness. And the assumption made by liberal intellectuals like Mr. Rajni Kothari was that since caste (and community) was the existential reality of Indian society, it was virtually inevitable that it become the operative political unit, and that the very integration of caste with the political process would erode its native strength. "It is not politics that gets caste-ridden; it is caste that gets politicised", he wrote in a celebrated essay. Common to both was the belief that the very modernity of the political experience would force a retreat on the backward consciousness of the Indian people.

Such mobilisation on the basis of community and caste did, of course, bring all those groups—the minorities, the lower castes and classes—into the political process which would either have been left out or would have taken much longer to get integrated with it. But then the very success of such mobilisation reinforced, instead of eroding all those primordial identities, and for good reason. Today, after four decades of experimenting with this ultra-modern polity, communal and caste identities are at their most assertive. The futility of the expectation that parties would abandon the very units which brought them to power somehow remained concealed from our political and academic leadership! Much against their hope, though as a consequence of their own choice, communalism has become an integral part of new India's state formation and the functioning of the state system caters to and promotes, in subtle or brazen ways, the logic of communal and caste solidarities. This happens even in the face of the weakening of these solidarities in social behaviour.

It would be argued that there is after all no getting away from community and caste as existential realities in India and hence their mobilisation for political support. Two points need to be made here in response. One that in India, as elsewhere, there are several existential realities besides community and caste, such as class division, regional and linguisite divisions, rural–urban divide, the rich–poor divide and so on and none of these has any more privileged claim to approximation to the Indian reality than any other. Therefore, the implicit assumption of community and caste mobilisation to the displacement of others seems highly problematic.

Secondly, it is important to make a distinction between an existential reality and a construction placed upon that reality. By accident of birth each one of us is born into a religio-cultural group and some part of it remains with us through life even when we consciously dilute or disown some or the other element of it. Even atheism does not eliminate all traces of a certain kind of cultural upbringing in the family, often conditioned by the enveloping religious milieu.

Thus a community identity is given to all of us by the name we bear, by the food we eat and by the festivals we celebrate as or with our children. But this does not become a communal identity unless some or the other party makes a specific appeal to it for mobilising political support and unless we respond to that appeal in competition with other appeals. Organising of riots is an extreme form of such mobilisation which seeks to transform community identity into communal identity. But it is also a common occurrence that in the midst of communal riots, devoutly religious individuals take many risks to extend protection and succour to those belonging to the other community involved in the riot; these individuals, cherishing their community identity, have clearly not allowed a communal construction to be placed upon it.

Lack history

The assumption of the inevitability of community or caste mobilisation for the working of Indian polity, to the displacement of other categories of mobilisation, is also not borne out by the history of that polity. Indeed, to date the most decisive electoral verdicts have emanated from issues other than community and caste and irrespective of which party brought up those issues. In 1967 the rising prices created an anti-Congress wave that wiped it out from all the states from Punjab to West Bengal; in 1971, the support for Mrs. Gandhi's Congress on the 'garibi hatao' call transcended the barriers of community and caste; 1977 saw the downfall of

Mrs Gandhi thanks to the Emergency. It was only in 1984 that Rajiv Gandhi was able to decisively play the Hindu card in a manner that it has never been played before or after, not even by the BJP, though we know how hard it tried. It is therefore open to each political party to make its choice from the range of categories that together constitute the Indian reality and to mobilise support with that category.

It does, however, appear all the more tragic that while our electorate has again and again demonstrated its ability to rise above communal and casteist mobilisation, it is the managers of the polity who are unwilling to give up their age-old constructions of the mind of the Indian masses, a mind they can only condescendingly conceive of as steeped in communal and caste identities. The Indian polity has indeed a long way to go to overcome its elite's backwardness.

The State and History

The Pioneer, 10.7.1992

The planned celebrations of the 450th birth anniversary of Emperor Akbar under the auspices of the Union Ministry of Human Resources Development brings into focus the relationship between the state and history all over again.

In a way, the hush-hush manner of planning the celebrations, which are scheduled to begin in October, but of which no news was allowed to leak out until first *The Times of India* and later *The Pioneer* reports unearthed it, itself suggests that more is involved in it than love for the late emperor. It clearly seems to be a fall-out of the attempt to be one up in the faction fight at the highest echelons of the Government.

If one asks a person going about in the street why does one study history, the most likely answer would be that it helps us rectify errors committed in the past. It is difficult to judge the veracity of this answer, for there is little evidence that societies do learn from their past mistakes and try not to repeat them. If they did, war would have become a thing of the past long ago.

But, quite apart from rectification, history does have another, more definitive, role: It serves as a source of legitimacy. Either as legitimacy for the state or for a movement of opposition to it, or, for that matter, an individual's or a group's search for space within the framework of the existing state system, more cynically designated as faction fight.

The Human Resource Development Ministry's

resurrection of Akbar's 450th birth anniversary at this juncture and the grand scale of the plans of celebrating the event do have a strong flavour of that search for legitimacy for one's own petty struggle. For at its best it continues and extends Mr. Arjun Singh's self-projection as the repository of secular nationalist ideals as against the Prime Minister's frequently projected ambiguity vis-i-vis the BJP's communalism. This projection might come handy in a showdown. It is fortuitous, therefore, to have been able to think of Akbar's anniversary at the appropriate moment.

All this raises some important questions: How far should the state's direct intervention in a kind of projection of history be considered legitimate, if at all? And, is it fair that lavish expenditure be undertaken for what would be a complete non-event for historians and non-historians alike at a time when the union government, acting through the UGC, has imposed heavy cuts on the libraries, laboratories and even the existing faculty positions on universities and colleges throughout the country for reasons of 'resource crunch'?

The most disastrous instance of state intervention in the writing and projetion of history has undoubtedly been the one made by the erstwhile Socialist regimes; it corrupted history and failed to legitimise the state. In India, the BJP would, left to itself, seek to reproduce the Socialist experiment in history-writing unmindful of its consequence.

Already, on a small scale, the BJP has started the process in Madhya Pradesh and Uttar Pradesh where it is 'rewriting' history textbooks for the schools. The only saving grace is the gross poverty of its kind of history.

The Congress regimes since Independence have not quite repeated the Socialist experiment, but as a characteristic half way, set down the parameters for history-writing, particularly at the textbooks level, namely that it must promote national integration and communal harmony, that is the Congress version of it. It has, therefore, been a somewhat milder version of the Socialist experiment, or the current BJP exercise.

Fortunately, as part of a functioning parliamentary

democracy, academic freedom, as well as freedom of the Press, with all their shortcomings, have become embedded in everyday consciousness of the Indian people. This freedom has allowed a respectable growth of history, largely as a non-conformist critical discipline in India, critical particularly of the state.

It is this autonomy of the discipline, its critical nature, which gets abbreviated with every intervention of the state—strong or mild. The abbreviation is not mitigated by the incorporation of professional historians in the effort, even when some of them have had a record of contemptuously rejecting every kind of state patronage in their younger, more revolutionary days.

The corrupting influence of such intervention becomes all the greater when it forms part of an immediate factional manoeuvre among politicians. It is, therefore, important for the profession of history to ask what is it that it would cherish more: Autonomy or state patronage?

It may, of course, be too much to expect the political leaders to realise that such patronage might bring to their side some historians, but not the legitimacy of history.

It is also important to talk about the expenditure involved, the amount of which is so closely guarded that press persons have only been left to make guesses about it.

At a time when the excuse of 'resource crunch' is handed out by the government for denying funds to virtually all educational and research institutions in the country, and when the need to enforce economy is doled out through duly televised ministerial speeches, what message would this presumably extremely expensive 'celebration', considering its scale, send out to those who might have had an inclination to actually believe the Government's statements?

Historical Wrongs

The Indian Express, 27.11.1998

The rise of the part-time historian

History-writing has been subject to several mutations the world over during the past half century or so. In the context of increasingly clearer admission that all forms of knowledge have historically grown through a cumulative, though not a concerted effort of all humanity, the creation of historical knowledge in each region is best seen as a part of evolving global patterns.

Seen in this perspective, Indian history writing has witnessed one major transition in the 1950s and 1960s and is poised for another in the 1990s. Down to the mid– 1950s, most history-writing and teaching was pivoted on ruling dynasties in ancient and medieval India, and around viceroys and governors in modern India. The divisions of ancient, medieval and modern itself was predicated upon dynastic shifts, though the terms were first used as late as 1903 by Stanley Lane-Poole: ancient India ended with AD 712, when Muhammad bin Qasim invaded India and medieval India, with the death of Aurangzeb in AD 1707.

Two elements shaped this perspective: the dominant inherited frame of history-writing in India's medieval centuries, and the dominant assumption everywhere that history was the creation of great deeds of great men.

The age-old view that ancient Indians had no sense of history has been ably contested by V.S. Pathak and

A.K. Warder in the 1960s and 1970s and by Romila Thapar in the 1990s. Warder, following "a really solid piece of constructive research, at last" by Pathak, affirms the existence of a historical consciousness in early India and reconstructs the social context of each.

The medieval centuries, however, posited an altogether different conception of history. The large number of court chronicles written in India in the Persian language envisioned history essentially as manifestation of human will, especially the ruler's will. The religious element also entered as a constituent of the ruler's nature. Thus the events of a reign manifest the ruler's personality. Hence, Alauddin Khalji conquered the Deccan because of his ambitious nature; Muhammad bin Tughlaq ended up a failure as ruler because his nature consisted of contradictory qualities; Akbar was tolerant towards the Hindus, for such was his nature and Aurangzeb was intolerant because of his natural religious dogmatism. This stands in contrast with medieval European historiography, where divine will is the sole cause of the occurrence of historical event. This is understandable; medieval Indian historians were all courtiers with varying shades of commitment to Islam; European historians were all ecclesiasts and saw history in unshaded theological colours.

The historical vision in general everywhere also centred on rulers, battles, empires and administration until very recent times. It was in protest against this approach that Marc Bloch and Lucien Febvre founded the celebrated French journal. *Annnales*, in 1929 in search of "a total history". In the 1930s and 1940s, dynastic history was giving way to comprehensive social and economic history. This was a major shift.

This shift came to Indian historiography substantively with the publication of D.D. Kosambi's *An Introduction to the Study of Indian History* in 1956. Kosambi, by profession a mathematician, was an assertive Marxist and the book altered the terms of historical discourse to class structure, class conflict, social and economic transformation. From the mid-1950s to around mid- 1980s the historical problematics centred on one or another aspect of this paradigm. And, very significant contributions were made to it by Irfan Habib and R.S. Sharma, among others, with their publications in 1963 and 1965. This was also the age of the growing influence of Marxism in intellectual endeavour as well as political and social spheres everywhere, for it was the age of Fidel Castro and Che Guevara, Vietnam and Ho Chi Minh. This was the age when an alternative vision of societal transformation pervaded the air.

In the 1990s, things have moved a long way off from that vision and have brought history-writing to yet another threshold. Once again newer problematics are being constituted: the history of ecology, of time and space, women, interpersonal relationships, perceptions and images, and so forth. This is happening in the community of historians around the world. It is, therefore, a sign of life among professional Indian historians that they have been sensitive and responsive to the waves of change in the constitution of historical knowledge, looking at it increasingly as a very complex rather than a monoconsal process. Religion too finds a place in this complexity.

Indian historiography has not only received these waves of knowledge but also contributed to them. The very fact of rewriting Indian history is a major contribution, for it alters perspectives on other parts of world history. But, more specifically, subaltern historiography in India is the object of respect and source of inspiration for many such studies in several other parts of the world and one does not have to be a subalternist oneself to appreciate this.

If history-writing then is a living rather than a dead discipline, sensitive to nuances, complexities and developing persectives, to view it exclusively as the story of religious combat and to view any complex explanation as a conspiracy of a few leftist historians who came to positions of power and thus propagated their false historiography is a charming demonstration of simplicity itself. Indeed, when the Marxist threshold in history-writing was crossed, its father-figure, D.D. Kosambi would not touch any government patronage with a barge pole; Nurul Hasan was not the minister of education, nor Satish Chandra the UGC chairman; nor had the ICHR yet been established. At any rate to reduce all these awesome changes in history writing everywhere in the world to the conspiracy of the leftists in India amounts to both looking at intellectual creativity simply as the result of state patronage and attributing to the state and the leftists an amount of power far beyond their capability.

To be fair, such few professional historians as the BJP has in its camp have seldom levelled these charges at least in public. They leave this task to the likes of Sita Ram Goel who, one learns, does full-time business for profit and part-time history for pleasure, and Arun Shourie who, too, one learns, does journalism for a living, specialising in the investigation of non-BJP persons' scandals and revelling in the discussion of virginity and hymens and has recently taken to proclaiming himself *the* historian and everyone else as 'historians'. Good luck to them.

A Crumbling Edifice

The Indian Express, 5.3.1999

Crime and the Indian Social order

The German sociologist-historian Norbert Elias had in a lifetime of exciting intellectual adventure explored many uncharted themes and created several innovative concepts before he died in 1991. 'Internalisation' was one such concept. Elias was not the first scholar to coin this term; it has indeed been used extensively and in different meanings. The most widespread use of the term has usually been in the sense of imbibing the ideas, notions and ideology of a class or a stratum that is alien or hostile to one's own or is at least its 'other'. Thus the peasantry internalising feudal value of loyalty, or the working class internalising the acquisitive ideology of capitalism or women internalising patriarchal notions of honour, etc. But this was not how Elias saw the term.

Elias was chiefly preoccupied with the contrast of the modern and the medieval worlds, which for him meant Europe. He emphasised that the economy of the ordering of modern society essentially lay in the replacement of the state's enforcement of laws and norms by their internalisation in each individual. Beginning with enforcement effected through punishment of infringement of laws in the form of fines, imprisonment, etc., modern society in Elias's vision has evolved into an organism where norms have both been universalised and so internalised by their citizens that the costs—economic, political and cultural—of supervision and enforcement by the state have considerably diminished. Whether it be in the sphere of traffic rules, office procedures, punctuality or the weight and quality of commodities on sale, payment of taxes or the management of crime, one can be fairly certain of adherence to publicly known laws and norms and there is scarce need to demostrate one's position or pelf to get things done.

Its obverse side is the awareness that position and pelf do not insulate one from punitive consequences following violation of norms or rules. This has allowed the state to withdraw itself increasingly from the sites of citizens' everyday life. A first-time Indian visitor to Europe is surprised at the car driver stopping, even when no police constable is around, to give way to the pedestrian who has priority in the right of way, or the cursory examination of one's passport at the entry or the exit point, as long as the visa does not arouse suspicion of forgery. Perhaps the most overpowering evidence of the economy of internalisation is the fact that Wellington, the capital of New Zealand, had the traffic-checking squad of two policemen in 1994!

It is true that the contrast between medieval and modern societies even in Europe in terms of one being organised exlusively or even predominantly around the use of force and other similarly around internalisation is a bit too stark for comfort. Medieval societies too had the acceptance of the legitimacy of the social order as an organising principle underneath the ever-present military force of the feudal lord; and even as modern society regulates itself through internalisation of the laws and norms, and the state gradually withdraws, the awareness of the state's presence in the background as the agency of punishment to ensure the orderly functioning of society remains in tact. But Elias was constructing a set of paradigms, sort of ideal types, to draw the dividing lines between what he perceived as characteristics of the medieval and the modern.

It is here much more than in the arena of science and

technology that present-day Indian society falls short of Elias's measure of 'modernity.' Even as independent India enshrined its cherished objective of equality before the law in the Consititution, the political process has been vitiated by two interrelated flaws: the inability of the state to command enough resources—more in terms of will than of material resources—to enforce the laws of the land; and hence public demonstration by the wealthy and the powerful that the laws could be defied and subverted with impunity. The consequence: loss of respect for the law, a loss that has gradually percolated to the lower ranks of society.

What increasingly appears as ever-growing lawlessness in our society is a reflection of the emulation of the behaviour of the elites as role models. Its concomitant consequence has been the desire to acquire wealth and power regardless of the means, as a guarantee of immunity from the reach of the law and norms. When Sanjay Nanda mowed down five young men under the wheels of his BMW and casually remarked, *log to girtey, padtey rahtey hain, yahan se chalo* (Ordinary mortals like these keep getting crushed all the time, therefore let us flee) and actually fled from the site of the accident, he and his friends, standing at the front ranks of India's most modern class, encapsulated the entire history of India's transition to 'modernity'. For he knew that he would get away with the crime, and he would have, if only his car's oil tank had not leaked. Just as a one-time socialist, former Prime Minister of the country, Chandra Shekhar is getting away with the acquisition of 600 acres of public land, with everyone looking the other way. Just as numerous ministers, chief ministers and prime ministers who have acquired crores have got away, what with all the inquiries pending against them.

Thus, if Elias's 'world' followed the path of enforcement of respect for the law and the gradual internalisation of this respect by all citizens, Indian elites have established contempt for the law as their distinctive characteristic and have thus established a model for emulation. The lawlessness that is manifesting itself in every-day murders and daylight robbery and, above all, the utter and public contempt of the law-enforcing agencies, i.e. the state, has its origin in the kind of lawlessness made into a fine art by independent India's political and economic elites. They also gradually become its targets.

In some ways, crime is therefore acquiring a degree of legitimacy bestowed upon it by the behaviour of the society's role models. Far from internalising compliance with the law, defiance of it is increasingly turning into a status symbol at all levels of society. This is happening as older institutions of social control of individual behaviour like the family, caste or community are breaking down and the state has not been allowed to establish its authority by its own managers. We are yet far away from realising that if compliance with the law can become pervasive, defiance of it too has similar dynamic.

The Stability Myth

The Indian Express, 4.10.1999

Politics, elections and governance

One cardinal and unique feature of Indian politics is that here every political party is in power and in the opposition at the same time. The BJP, Congress, the JD, the CPI (M) are all in power is some states and in opposition in some others. Socially too, almost all castes and community groups are at the helm of affairs in some states and at the receiving end in others. This makes Indian polity a compulsively federal one. It is understandable, therefore, that a melange of conflicting interests and issues should mark its functioning and should define electoral battles at each election time. It would also perhaps explain the instability that inheres in the very working of parliamentary democracy which is the polity's operative instrument. One aspect of the instability is the frequency with which governments fall.

Has this inherent instability been necessarily detrimental to India's economic development and political maturing? Let us examine the question first contra-factually, from the opposite end, as it were. In the half century-old history of the working of parliamentary democracy in India, there have inevitably been long periods of stability, as well as conditions on which prolonged stability is premised (such as a decisive majority for a single party in the Lok Sabha); there have also been periods of considerable instability due to an uncertain verdict returned by the electorate. In the first three elections, between 1952 and 1962, the Congress was returned with comfortable majorities and fall of governments did not loom large on the political scene, except for the dismissal of the Communist government in Kerala in 1958 under Article 356 by Jawaharlal Nehru.

The dream of rapid economic development following the path of 'a socialistic pattern of society'—a typically Nehruvian compromise between what were then perceived as antagonistic developmental paths of free enterprise and the Soviet brand of socialism—had on one hand created a miserable annual growth of around 3 per cent, derisively referred to as the 'Hindu rate of growth' and, on the other, led to a massive popular anger over rising prices in 1967 that swept off all the Congress governments from Punjab to West Bengal except at the Centre. The long stability had for sure allowed the nation to heal its wounds following the country's tragic partition; but it had proved no sweet recipe for economic development.

In 1971 India Gandhi's call for *garibi hatao* won her a massive mandate, perhaps a bit too massive for comfort, but this and her decisive intervention in the coming into existence of Bangladesh in the following year did not prevent the tide of economic discontent. The Railway strike of 1974 was its most visible manifestation. The mandate ended in the imposition of the Emergency in 1975. In 1984, Rajiv Gandhi won an even more massive mandate than his mother and promised to usher in the 21st century which in popular perception meant a clean, transparent government that would bring about rapid economic growth. Three years on, his government was in a shambles.

In the states too, the CPI(M) has created a history of sorts by providing the longest lasting stable government in independent India's history—Jyoti Basu has been chief minister for 22 long years. Has the stability of the West Bengal Government brought the state to the forefront of the country's economic, political or social landscape? On all accounts the prolonged stability of government there has been accompanied by a low level economic equilibrium. Politically, the Left has remained lodged at the margins and quite content with that position. The BJP-Shiv Sena, too, have ruled Maharashtra for five years by now without a threat of fall or dismissal; this fact, however, has in no measure either created an economic miracle, reduced social turmoil, or improved the law and order scenario in the state.

On the other hand it was the minority government of Narsimha Rao which willingly or unwillingly brought about a break with the legacy of economic policies of the past and allowed a degree of liberalisation; the result has been some departure from the lines drawn by the Hindu rate of growth. And all reports on the economy in the current phase have indicated an upward movement in the past three months or so; these are the months of a government which had lost the confidence of the Lok Sabha— in other words a most unstable and crippled government.

There does not appear then any necessary link between stable govenment and economic growth. The converse is perhaps not true either: from this one can hardly infer that an unstable government is essential for economic growth or social stability. But making an issue of stability and implicitly blaming the illiterate Indian electorate for not providing the conditions for it does not get validated by history. Considering that there is now virtually a consensus on economic policies from BJP to CPI(M) with the Congress in between, the assumption of political power by one party or another for whatever length of time should make little difference to the question of economic growth. There is, in fact, a growing disjuncture between economy and politics.

In some ways the Indian polity has the resilience to initiate measures of economic growth and political maturing. Economic statistics apart, those of us who have grown to adulthood in the 1950s and 1960s would recall with distaste the picture of almost every finance minister, with his begging bowl, making a beeline to the West, especially the US, to ask for aid under one pretext or another. Much of India still remains desperately poor, but the begging bowl and the finance minister are no longer inseparable. The maturing of Indian parliamentary democracy, too, with all its shortcomings and flaws, does give one some sense of satisfaction.

Indeed, the Indian electorate has always responded enthusiastically every time issues over-riding caste, community or other narrow affiliations have been posed to it as in 1967 (price rise), 1971 (*garibi hatao*), 1977 (the Emergency), and so on. It is always the absence of such issues that brings to the fore the electorate's caste and community loyalties. As in the election now under way, an election in which the absence of issues on all sides seems to be the most visible issue.

The failure then does not lie in the structure of polity and in the political process; it has been one of good governance which comes with a vision, transparency and the impartial enforcement of laws. Good governance is not predicated upon one or other form of government: presidential, parliamentary, or any combinations of these. There are numerous states in the world today that have experimented with virtually lifelong presidencies: they have had stability but not good governance.

Ray of Hope in Kashmir?

The Hindu, 10.6.2002

In the course of the last few days, two momentous stories were published in the newspapers in the context of Jammu and Kashmir: the Prime Minister, Atal Behari Vajpayee's solemn assurance in Srinagar that the coming Assembly elections in the State will be completely free and fair to the extent of being a turning point in its history; and the report of the survey conducted by the British market research organisation, Mori International, on behalf of a human rights group, that a huge majority of the people in the State wanted peace and to stay with India rather than to go with Pakistan.

For appreciating the significance of the Prime Minister's statement, it is essential to go a long distance into history. Way back in 1947, when Kashmir had the option of throwing its lot with either Pakistan or India, the one attraction Pakistan could hold out was the bond of Islam. It was unclear then which way the economies of the two newborn states would go and what place each would carve out for itself in the emerging world scenario. The one plus point India had on its side was the promise of a secular, democratic Government, based on the parliamentary system, whose legitimacy was premised upon free and fair elections. Clearly then, in choosing to side with India, Kashmir announced its preference for secularism and democracy over its religious identity. However, while in the rest of India parliamentary democracy's movement towards maturity through the zigzag of booth-capturing and bogus voting, money and muscle power, began to emerge from shaded zones to the zone of clarity, Jammu and Kashmir was one State where this process was firmly denied any locus from the word go. The underlying premise of the denial was an overarching suspicion of the Kashmiri people, i.e. the Muslims. The assumption that given an opportunity, the valley's Muslims would desert to Pakistan and take the territory with them was the unstated reason why they would have to do without the luxury of free and fair elections. This assumption kept the State and its people scissored off from the mainstream developments in the rest of the country. It was an assumption totally shared by India's political class, the diversity of its other hues notwithstanding.

In the 1970s and 1980s, when the political alignments in the country were undergoing major mutations and the entire range of Opposition parties was tasting the fruits of government power, one experiment among others then in the offing was what was known as the Opposition Conclave. This involved leaders of major parties, in power in States but in opposition to the Congress government at the Centre, seeking to form an all-India coalition as an alternative to the Congress. Farooq Abdullah, along with Jyoti Basu and M. Karunanidhi, was a very prominent player in this game. The Government at the Centre with a large vision should have greatly welcomed this denouement, for more than even his father, Dr. Abdullah's attempt would have led to the integration of Jammu and Kashmir's politics with that of the rest of India; that in turn would have proved to be the most dependable capping of the region's separatist assertions. But in conformity with D.K. Barooah's momentous expression of sycophancy, 'Indira is India', Indira Gandhi did actually believe that if one was against her one was against India. The Opposition Conclave then by its very nature was anti-India and Dr. Abdullah was more anti-India than the others. He must therefore be shown the door, never mind if he had been elected in the only free and fair election ever held in Jammu and Kashmir in 1978 when Morarji Desai was Prime Minister.

The rest of the story is known, if faintly remembered. Through one of the most audacious and contemptuous violations of the norms of parliamentary democracy in the history of independent India, Indira Gandhi dismissed Dr. Abdullah's government and in his place installed his brother-in-law, Ghulam Mohammad Shah. This regime touched new lows in corruption. More than the financial corruption, it was the political message that was loud and clear: free and fair elections be damned; if you wish to remain in power in Jammu and Kashmir, cower before the Centre. To top it, Indira Gandhi played the overt communal card in the 1983 election in the State, primarily in preparation for the 1984 national elections.

Dr. Abdullah accepted the message and established links with the Congress, with Rajiv Gandhi in particular. That not only put paid to the Opposition Conclave, it greatly eroded Dr. Abdullah's own legitimacy as Jammu and Kashmir's, especially the Valley's, political leader, which was predicated upon opposition to the Centre, much as the politics in several other States has been and still remains. West Bengal, for one.

Ironically, the last elections held in Jammu and Kashmir in 1997 under the aegis of Dr. Abdullah's government reached a high water mark of being unfree and unfair on all counts. This admission is implied in the Prime Minister's assurance of the next elections being completely free and fair.

If the Indian state went back on the one promise it had made to Kashmir, which was the basis of its integration with India, i.e. secularism and true democracy, then Kashmir turned to the assertion of the one identity whose legitimacy was not subject to manipulation by the Indian state: its Muslim identity.

The high degree of the alienation of the Valley's Muslims from India becomes intelligible in the context of the complete lack of trust in them; this was an alienation almost thrust upon them. Pakistan could not have created or sought a more conducive context for carrying out its objectives in the Valley.

It is in this background that the Prime Minister's

undertaking of conducting a completely free election in the State becomes momentous. For, this alone has the potential to give Kashmir what it had sought to begin with, i.e. real democracy; this is one thing Pakistan's state cannot still give it, when it is unable to give it to its own people.

Just when one was beginning to feel that even a genuinely free and fair election in Jammu and Kashmir might come too late and that things have moved too far away from the starting point, the British survey comes as a breath of fresh air.

All the violence and long drawn alienation has still not killed the faint hope that Kashmir will stay with India. However, clearly more than the Prime Minister's assurance at a press conference is required to give hope that the election would indeed be genuine and not fraudulent. Is our political system up to it?

Let Every Truth Become Suspect

TOI, 23.7.2005

PM's speech questioned the certitudes of history

History in the end gives you a way of looking at things. Ways, in fact, with no finality and no ultimate objective truth vesting in any of them. Time was when the predominant perspective was constituted in adversarial categories: Class versus class, imperialism versus colony, dark versus white races, one religion versus another, and more recently women versus men, or for that matter, continuity versus change. Each of the categories comprised a complete unity in itself standing in total opposition to its other, with no shared spaces between them.

But times change and so does one's historical vision. Today, the certitudes embedded in the oppositional categories have become vulnerable and interaction in lieu of opposition has become a far more seductive proposition. Prime Minister Manmohan Singh's speech at Oxford is indeed attuned to this interactive perspective, regardless of whether or not he is keeping abreast of developments in the academic discipline which is not his own.

The significant mutation that has occurred does not quite eliminate the old antagonisms between imperialism and colony, between continuity and change and does not wish away the exploitation that had hitherto explained history. But the relationship has begun to be seen as a process in which both sides affected each other deeply.

And this happens independently of the intentions of either side. Karl Marx's famous observation about the enormous suffering being inflicted on Indian people by the British colonial regime, yet breaking down the shackles that had kept India in a state of complete stagnation for all its past, is derived from a very flimsy knowledge of Indian history; it yet makes a methodological departure in looking at historical processes not in terms of intentions of dramatis personae but in terms of the results of their actions, or objective results as devout Marxists will fondly describe it.

It therefore, becomes unimportant that the British built the railways with the intention of intensifying their exploitation of India (did they ever claim that the railways were built to promote national integration?) or that they introduced English language education to create a stratum of babus for keeping the costs of running the administration low; what remains important is the long-term consequences of these actions.

One of the effects of the changing perspective on history is that the decline and fall of empires is seen not so much as the result of a catastrophic collision with an outside force but as a culmination of acculturation within.

Thus the Mughal empire collapsed not because of the dogmatic religious policy of Aurangzeb and the devastating Hindu reaction to it, as Jadunath Sarkar had taught us, nor owing to the rebellion of the impoverished peasantry against the ever-exploitative state, as Irfan Habib had so eloquently argued in 1963. It collapsed when the mansabdars and zamindars, integrated within the empire, mobilised resources thus obtained and sought to carve out their own independent regimes, much as deputy CEOs of corporate organisations set up their own businesses today.

Much of the parent institution inheres in the new set-up even when new morés and methods evolve. The leaders of India's freedom struggle, too, had mobilised organisational, legal, ideological and intellectual resources from their education in England to bring the empire to its knees. The issue is not of continuity versus change but one of continuity *and* change.

Historians today have raised serious questions about the earlier dividing lines, in particular 1765, that had marked the traditional date for the onset of colonialism. They visualise the decades between 1750s and 1830s as a period of flux when a lot of adoption, adaptation and appropriation of each other's assets and values occurred. William Dalrymple has also shown, with great diligence, the same phenomenon in the cultural arena in the same period in his *White Mughals.*

Indeed, the very title of his book seeks a shared space between two opposing categories. The British dominance in the relationship is dateable to a long century after this period. The institutions that still run a major part of India's political, judical, military and bureaucratic administration and even its economy and academia were also created in this period, accompanied at the same time by the highest intensity of exploitation.

Manmohan Singh's Oxford speech thus has the finesse of not counterposing one aspect of the consequences of colonialism in India against the other, but taking all of it as an ensemble the way Marx had done in 1853. Knowingly or unknowingly, the PM was also treading the path that historians of various hues have been exploring recently. As the eminent Urdu poet, Faiz Ahmed Faiz, said: "*Har haqeeqat majaaz ho jaaye*" (Let every established truth become suspect). It is only through this self-questioning that we shall be able to renew ourselves.

Yesterday Once More

TOI, 17.7.2008

How many historic blunders will our comrades commit?

The story we heard as young students back in the early 1950s was that even as CPI's student volunteers were marching in a procession against the British regime following the Quit India call by Mahatma Gandhi, Arun Bose, head of the party's youth brigade went running after them asking them to stop and turn back, shouting: 'The party line has changed, comrades'! The party itself and its subsequent fragments, including the bigger one—the CPM—have never quite accepted it as a blunder, or even as a minor mistake. Indeed they invariably offer a very laboured explanation of the World War having turned into a 'people's war' with the Soviet Union having intervened on the Allies' side. Others, however, never let go of an opportunity to remind them of their 'betrayal' of the nation at that critical hour: comrades usually fall silent whenever this reminder is thrown at their face.

Come independence in 1947, and before the celebrations had subsided, the party, then led by B.T. Ranadive, a 1940s version of Prakash Karat, very learned in Marxist theory, completely unfamiliar with the notion of moderation as well as of practical politics, voiced the slogan: "Yeh azadi jhoothi hai; janata abhi bhi bhookhi hai". He launched an armed uprising from Telengana to overthrow the bourgeois regime which, according to the party, had been placed in power by the colonial regime in a conspiracy against the rising tide of communist revolution. The uprising was suppressed brutally, as the state always does when faced with a threatening challenge.

The price paid by faithful believers in the call of revolution was massive. But they were ordinary workers, always dispensable for a worthy cause. The leaders were put in jail and released. Even this was never formally achnowledged as a blunder, although the replacement of Ranadive with Ajoy Ghosh and the resolution to participate in parliamentary politics "to help complete the bourgeois democratic revolution" as a step towards achieving "a people's democratic revolution" was an implicit admission enough.

Things worked smoothly for a while. So long as workers went on strikes and held gheraos and dharnas and simultaneously party candidates contested elections, the state was not really threatened. Indeed, the state welcomed the absorption of the challenging agency into its fold through election of governments in the states. So complete was the absorption that in the next bout of a serious challenge from the outside, i.e. the Naxalite movement, the CPI and CPM became its chief targets. Nor need we forget that the only party other than the Congress which whole-heartedly welcomed the imposition of the Emergency by Indira Gandhi was the CPI.

But by now a radical metamorphosis of the communist movement in India had occurred: its role would henceforth remain strictly confined to the four walls of parliamentary politics. With coalition politics becoming the new norm, a great opportunity came its way in 1998 when there was the possibility of Jyoti Basu heading a coalition government. Karat is known to be the one dead set against this happening and succeeded in enacting what Basu later called a "historic blunder". Basu was not lamenting the denial of the PM's chair to him; he saw the results of that denial in BJP's subsequent rise to power for six long years. It was as a corrective to that blunder that he and another 'practical' politician in the CPM leadership, Harkishen Singh Surjeet, helped forge a Left-UPA coalition following the 2004 elections.

That coalition is in a shambles now, because Karat, who has learnt his Marxism in a British University and JNU, is obviously unmindful of minor headaches like paving the way for the BJP's return. Ranadive was fortunate in that he did not have to choose from among many enemies: there was no BJP or its predecessor. The Congress was his single enemy. Karat has made his choice. The Congress still remains his single enemy and if he has to traverse the path in the company of the BJP, so be it. He finds the very communal reason given by Mayawati for denunciation of the nuclear deal as anti-Muslim laudable, even as several highly respected Muslim bodies have refused to link Islam with opposition to the nuclear deal.

Nor has he any problem with all the crores Mayawati has made in the past few years. Mayawati's declared intention—and the practice of it—to capture power and hold on to it regardless of whoever is willing to support her, including the BJP, is of no concern to Karat either. These small details must be ignored for the higher cause of bringing to heel a government which spent four years accommodating some reasonable and some grossly unreasonable demands placed before it with a 'do it or else' command.

One can imagine the BJP leaders chuckling under their breath about the help the Left is rendering them. If the Left under the leadership of Karat does go all the way and the BJP does stage a return to power at the Centre, there is no doubt that one more senior CPI or CPM leader will call it one more historic blunder, and wait for the next one to happen.

How do we understand feudalism?

Dawn, Karachi, 16.5.2008

I HAVE been following the very interesting debate on the question of feudalism in Pakistan in the pages of *Dawn.* I think one among several problems with the notion of feudalism is that it was conceptualised long after its demise in Western Europe and in the wake of the rise of its adversary, i.e. capitalism. It was thus constituted not in its own terms but as the 'other' of capitalism. It thus became a residual category — inclusive of everything that capitalism was supposedly not.

If capitalism was progressive and rational, feudalism was backward-looking and marked by superstition. If capitalism was driven by ceaseless technological and economic dynamism, feudalism was stagnant. If capitalism was based upon wage labour, which was a purely economic form of coercion, feudalism was fundamentally characterised by non-economic or extra-economic coercion. Combined with the post-Enlightenment derision of the Middle Ages as the Dark Ages, marked by superstition, subservience, stagnation etc. etc., feudalism thus came to be a term of extensive, indeed comprehensive, abuse.

History, however, does not quite substantiate this derision. Economically and technologically it was a period of enormous dynamism. Indeed, the great historian of France, Marc Bloch, in his landmark work, *Feudal Society,* divided the period into the first and the second feudal ages and observed that even as the society lived by a consciousness of changelessness, so profound and pervasive was change that if an inhabitant of one feudal age were to visit the other, he would not have been able to recognise it.

Technology of agricultural production had evolved, greatly improving the productivity of land and labour; the three-field system had by and large replaced the two-field system; agricultural production itself had expanded to the arable vast forests in eastern Europe; new and better food crops were now being cultivated. Population had grown rapidly, releasing peasants, who were characteristically tied to the land, into an emerging mobile labour market; and so forth.

Indeed, later European historians of the second half of the 20th century had even become wary of using the term 'feudalism' for the medieval society, for it appeared to them to be far too tightly structured. And I speak of frontline historians such as Georges Duby, Jacques Le Goff and Aaron Gurevich, among many others.

Culturally too, the European Middle Ages gave us some of the immortal works of art whether in architecture, or painting, music or poetry. The same can be said of the Middle Ages everywhere: India, China, Japan, the Arab-Muslim world. But then, the period was also one of enormous exploitation, repression and subordination of one or another section of society by those who had command over the resources, something again true of all ages, including our own.

But the image of feudalism as the repository of all that was oppressive, regressive, superstitious, has survived. One can read all these abuses and much more in some recent writings. It is this image that is mobilised in an attempt to rise to the rational modernity, which notion too is given to us by post-Enlightenment Europe, just as the notion of feudalism was. That is the problem: we are trapped in a discourse that is not of our making, whichever way we might turn.

The terms of debate are really not of our own creation, as

it were. And clearly these are all heavily loaded terms, each carrying a baggage even as they appear to us as merely descriptive of an 'objective' situation.

We are thus faced with a situation of austere academic analysis of feudalism leading us in one direction and the need for its mobilisation for political agitation into another.

Can we find a compatible space between the two? I think it involves much harder work especially on the part of academics than the easy way out of falling back upon a convenient and familiar term. It is important to recognise that the classic Marxist definition of capitalism as 'generalised commodity production where labour is a commodity' marks its idealised, purest form, its ultimate goal; prior to arriving at that purest form, capitalism can combine all kinds of not only pre-capitalist labour uses, but virtually any kind of social structure.

The cotton farmers of the South in the US in the 19th century were no less capitalist because they were employing slave labour on their farms. Japan is among the frontline capitalist economies of the world today, next only to the US, but in terms of its social structure, especially its subjection of women, it is way behind many of even the developing countries; and the 'feudal' value of loyalty is still a strong tie that binds many of the employees to their companies even for generations. All of these do not contravene its character as a capitalist economy and society.

It is therefore important to seek to understand each scenario in concrete terms before we take the easy resort to carry-bag categories.

Walking the Higher Ed Elephant

IE, 30.6.2009

Flexibility shouldn't be the exception, it must be the norm

The enormous significance of the nehruvian vision for higher education in India is now coming home to us, as India earns its niche in the 21st-century world. With all its many shortcomings and failures, it still remains true that at the higher level of teaching and research in almost all brances, be it natural sciences, medicine, social sciences or literature, Indian universities have enabled their students to find placement in the best of institutions any-where in the world. Yet, there is still a very long way to to.

Having taught history for 44 years at Delhi University's Hindu Collelege (where incidentally Kapil Sibal was briefly my younger department colleague some 40 years ago) and JNU, I can perhaps claim a little initmacy with some of the problems that inhabit higher education. Chief among these is not financial constraints: it is the problem of resistance to experimentation onself, coupled with an even greater reluctance to let one's students engage in it. In other words, the chief problem is intellectual inertia. Thus, despite everything, teaching and research in India has not produced one overarching concept or theory, or one invention that has led to a paradigm shift in virtually any branch of knowledge—or, for that matter, in governing humanity's daily life. Our systems are too hidebound for that. G. Parthasarathim JNU's founding Vice-Chancellor, didn't share this narrowness; his vision, to allow its students and faculty presicous space for freedom and intellectual adventure, still survives in patches, and is what has earned it such high respect.

Yet, even in institutions like JNU, the space was highly constricted and seems to have become more so over time. Theoretically, for example, a student can seek admission to any dicipline in JNU irrespective of one's previous disciplinary background, if one is able to clear the admission test; and there have been cases where such boundaries were indeed crossed. But on the whole the ratio of such cross-discipline admissions would not exceed a fraction of a per cent. The boundaries ge tighter one admission has been given. The faculties are mailny uni-disciplinary, as are the courses; and reaching out to courses in other disciplines is tightly controlled. Yet, wherenver these controls are relaxed, the results are spactacular. Let me cite two such examples.

Ramya Srinivisan was a young lecturer in English literature in Miranda House when she sought admission to the PhD course in history at JNU with the proposal to work on the evolution of the many legends of Rani Padmini of Cittor over several centuries and in different regions. She could not convince the Centre for Historical Studies that, given her back-ground in English, she would be able to deal with the sbject with competence. Luckily, the Centre for English was more relaxed wand admitted her, to be jointly supervised by Professor Minakshi Mukherjee (later Professor J.G.V. Prasad) and me. Today an associate professor of history, she is the author of an outstanding book on the subject, that dexterously combines her expertise in literary criticism and historical contextualisation. Sumit Ganguli was doing his Master's in medieval history and wanted to opt for a course in human rights. Asked the faculty; what has human rights got to do with medieval history? But somehow he got permission. He pursued the subject further—coming back to Chennai as UNHRC representative.

Thus, just a little lecway in letting students go beyound

the strict rules can produce competence of very high calibre. Our students at the univerisy level deserve more, rather that less, such flexiblity. And this flexiblity needs to be insitutionalised.

But a prime requisite of greater flexiblity is the teacher's constant engagement in updating as well as widening their own knowlege. Failure to do so, even for just three-to-five years, can leave one a long distance behind, given the rapidity with which knowledge in each discipline is changing. With the very impressive improvement in teahcers' salaries recently, it is the libraries and the laboratories that call for immediate and focused attention. This, and some system of rewards for excellence—which necessarily also implies absence of rewards for the laggards. Nothing damages a system more that its inability to distinguish between energy and lethargy. It is a shame that we do not have a mechanism in place even for ensuring regular taking of one's classes, much less of updating one's knowledge. It is hard to imangine greater inhumanity than for a teacher to pass on out dated knowlege to one's unsuspecting students.

With sibal in charge, expectations are high, hoping for radical change. It will be a great tribute to Nehru's vision to raise the system once again to the stature which he had accorded it Raising of teachers' salaries is one major welcome step in that direction; the stage is ready for the many others.

II. Facets of Communalism

Communalism and Indian Politics

Economic and Political Weekly, Vol. XVIII, No. 31, 24.9.1983

Communalism, in its most commonly perceived form, is the phenomenon of religious differences between groups often leading to tension, and even rioting, between them. In its not-so violent manifestation communalism amounts to discrimination against a religious group in matters of employment or education or whatever. By the same logic secularism seeks to negate discrimination and tension with equal degree of respect in private and public life and by recognising equal title of citizens belonging to all religious groups to participate in and benefit from the country's progress. It is in this sense that secularism has been adopted as the keynote of Indian state policy since Independence by successive governments.

It can perhaps be argued that this communalism/ secularism dichotomy, far from being dichotomous, in fact belongs to a range of analysis the categories of which are themselves essentially communal. In this dichotomy the locus of communalism is placed at the point of tension, either in the form of discrimination or in the exteme form of a riot. But tension—let us say a riot—is merely an overt manifestation of a phenomenon which also manifests itself at its other end in a silent, almost imperceptible, form and the two together constitute a spectrum in which communalism could get expressed at any point. Clearly any explanation of the phenomenon of communalism must take into account this entire specturm.

A society is not merely what it is: an important element in the functioning of a society is the perception of it by its constituents. The basis of a communalist perception is that social analysis in which communities constitute the categories. Once political parties perceive Indian society in terms of communities, in terms of Hindus as Hindus and Muslims as Muslims, etc., they can adopt one of the following two strategies: they can either seek to consolidate general support for themselves by emphasising the need for peaceful co-existence between different communities as equal citizens of the country and by trying to impart a sense of security of life and property to the minorities, the Hindu–Muslim bhai-bhai syndrome; or they can opt for support in a particular community by overly drawing the image of another community's hostility to it or even by organising riots against that other community. Both these strategies originate in the same social analysis in terms of communities and are therefore integrally linked to each other. Indeed both these strategies are interdependent: winning over the minorities to one's side by appearing to be their defender (as has been the Congress strategy) can be most effective only when there is a live threat hanging over the minorities' heads (such as the RSS threat to the Muslims); on the other hand, projection of 'defence' of the minorities as 'excessive concessions' is equally essential for creating prejudice against them. It is thus that the two strategies merge in a continuum; the Congress and the RSS, far from being each other's alternative, constitute the extremes of this continuum. It is also thus that the Congress has been able to supplant the BJP without a murmur as the bastion of Hindu support in Jammu and Punjab, for it is not very hard to shift one's position ever so slightly within this continuum and displace another occupant of that position.

The familiar comunalism secularism dichotomy is in fact a legacy of the national movement, characterised by the Muslim League–Congress antagonism. The politics of the two were based upon the recognition of the existence of separate communities though their strategies were clearly different. Since the basic assumption was common, it often permitted an easy transition from one to the other; it also often brought them to a common meeting ground by a slight shift in each other's direction, apart from facilitating quick changes in individual loyalties or even permiitting dual loyalties. Conceptually nationalism and communalism shared much with each other even when historically they stood as each other's negation.

The communalism/secularism dichotomy therefore is conceptually questionable even though empirically it is extremely significant. Conceptually an analysis in terms of social classes rather than communities is the true negation of communalism. The concept of class trancends, and stands in opposition to the communal, regional, caste or linguistic identities. It needs to be emphasised that class analysis is not mere economic analysis, though of course the economic aspect is very important in it. It is also worth stating that it is not poverty or absolute scarcity of resources that leads to communal groupings and tensions; it is on the other hand an expansion of opportunities that creates such tensions, for opportunities can never expand sufficiently to satisfy everyone's demands; and yet they create considerable upheavals by widening the gulf between groups.

To come back to the concept of class as the alternative to community based analysis. While it is true that ideally class transcends communities, etc. it is equally true that political parties swearing by class ideology also eagerly enter into alliances with patently communal parties such as the Muslim League in Kerala, the Akali Dal in Punjab and the erstwhile Jan Sangh in U.P. and Bihar (in 1967), alliances dictated by compulsions of parliamentary politics. At their best the Left parties' alliances with parties of the minority communities have been justified on the ground that it is majority communalism alone that is capable of turning into a fascist threat; minority communalism is a defensive reaction and is therefore not as dangerous. At their worst such alliances point to opportunism of the Left parties. Having said that it is necessary to recognise that communalism is not central to the politics of the Left parties as it is to that of others, all of which think in terms of communities.

At any rate the fact that even parties with a class-based ideology fall prey to compromises with communal parties strongly suggests that so long as we work the present polity we have to live with communalism. In its violent form of riots it can be handled effectively as a law-and-order problem at one locus and not-so effectively at another; giving concessions to the aggrieved party at one place might lead to the subsidence of passions there although that itself might reinforce communal demands for more concessions elsewhere; it might also build up resentment in the rival community. This unfortunately is the rather limited range of remedies to the communal problem in the given set-up.

Alternative to Communalism

Frontline, 24 Jan. – 6 Feb. 1987

The unexpected ferocity of the recent communal tension in Karnataka, a region without a history of such tension, coming on the heels of the intense communal situation in Punjab and Gujarat, would necessarily point to the fragility of Indian secularism. The retreat of secularism is perceived as the advance of communalism, for the two are usually seen in a dichotomous relationship. The common explanation that it is the politicians who exploit religious differences for making political gains is true enough at a simple level. However, implicit in this explanation is the assumption that if only politicians could forego narrow personal or party interests and if religion could be separated from the sphere of politics, communalism would be eliminated from the Indian polity. But how is it that such noble sentiments fail to inspire politicians and the religious and the political spheres fail to get demarcated? A perspective capable of explaining this failure would emerge if we re-examine the received wisdom about the communalism–secularism dichotomy.

A recently articulated emphasis by social scientists as well as politicians has sought to distinguish the specifically Indian notion of secularism from the one that evolved in Europe. In Europe, secularism has come to signify the State's indifference to matters religious; in India on the other hand secularism means the very opposite, namely the State's respect for all religions. Communalism, also a specifically Indian phenomenon, is in turn seen as championing the cause of one's own religious group, often in hostility with other groups. If communalism creates political and economic tensions from out of religious differences, secularism preaches the doctrine of religious and political harmony. 'Hindu-Muslim bhai-bhai' was nearly universally the dominant theme of medieval devotional literature, popular among the masses. This had a laudable effect. Even in situations when the medieval 'Muslim' State was engaged in life-and-death political conflicts with various religious groups— the Jat and Maratha Hindus, the Sikhs and the Shia rulers of Bijapur and Golconda—peace prevailed at the social level. Indeed, communal rioting, which is such a dismal feature of everyday life in India today, was virtually unknown in the medieval centuries.

Mass mobilisation

This was partly because political mobilisation in medieval India was to a far less extent based on mass mobilisation; and to the extent it was so based, it had the State as its target rather than another community. Partly also, the absence of any conceptual alternative to the category of community and the category of social analysis in medieval centuries allowed for the rather limited choice of either promoting communal conflict or communal harmony. The former was achieved by highlighting the points of tension between leaders of communities and the latter by underlining their common features. Clearly both the phenomena inhered in the coexistence of communities.

It is from this legacy of relative communal calm at the social level, even in the midst of political conflict, that the commonly accepted Indian version of secularism seeks to derive its legitimacy.

There is, however, a problem, originating in the use of these medieval categories for analysing and operating a far more complex 20th-century society, when a much wider choice of categories is possible. If all we can think of doing after a communal riot is to lead a procession comprising members from several communities and shout slogans like 'Hindu-Muslim bhai-bhai' or its other variants, however laudable its objective, we must be prepared to take a hard look at our experience and ask whether it has stemmed the tide of communalism. The answer is unfortunately in the negative; on the eve of Independence, the 'secular' opposition to the communal demand for the partition of India had to give way, and now, four decades after Independence, the situation on this front is grim. Clearly the specific Indian notion of secularism has proved and is now proving unequal to its adversary in the fierce struggle Why is this so?

Point of tension

In the communalism secularism dichotomy, communalism is identified at a point of tension, at a point where either there is discrimination in favour or against a person or a group for reasons of religious affinity, or in an extreme case, where there is communal rioting. The absence of such tension is understood to indicate secularism. The problem with this understanding is that it identifies communalism only at a single locus and in only one manifestation, namely that of overt tension; communalism in reality comprises a range of positions and expresses itself in violent as well as silent manifestations.

In its silent manifestation, communalism inheres in the very category of social analysis and political operation. Once a political party analyses Indian society in terms of Hindus. Muslims, Sikhs and the like, it could follow either of the two strategies; it could seek to consolidate support for itself among all communities by harking to the 'Hindu-Muslim bhai-bhai' vision; this would imply reassuring the minorities about the security of their economic interests and cultural and religious identity; else, it could seek to be the representative of the economic and cultural interests of one community. This in turn would mean overstating the assumed hostility of another community or communities to that of one's own. The first strategy is the hallmark of the working of such parties as the Congress and the Janata Party; the second that of the BJP, the Muslim League, the Akali Dal and the like.

We have commonly come to accept these two strategies as exclusive and alternative to each other. In effect, since both operate with the community as the basic unit, each shares much with the other. Hence, far from being alternatives to each other they together constitute a continuum, comprising the entire range of communal positions and their various manifestations. Within the continum each party could follow a strategy different from those of others; but the continuum allows them an interchange of positions and a return to one's own original stance. Indeed, it allows any one party to follow more than one strategy simultaneously. We have had an excellent demonstration of all these points recently. The Congress (I) first wiped out the BJP from the Jammu and Kashmir Assembly in the 1983 elections by overtly championing the cause of the State's Hindus. The success delighted it. The strategy was repeated on a much larger scale in the 1984 parliamentary elections with far more devastating results. The BJP on its part, has briefly experimented with a 'secular' image, though it has now resiled to its safer 'Hindu' constituency. The Janata Party allows one of its leading lights, Syed Shahabuddin, to make one grossly communal plea after another while itself sticking to its 'secular' strategy.

It is thus that communalism and secularism blend with each other in building the economy and working the polity of modern India. Communal rioting as the extreme manifestation of communalism, occurs most frequently in the economically most advanced locales: Ahmedabad, Baroda, Hyderabad, Moradabad and of course Punjab, pointing to the inevitable conclusion that communalism, far from being a sign of backwardness, has become a concomitant of the particular pattern of India's economic development. Similarly, the operation of the very modern polity with which India has experimented since Independence, namely parliamentary democracy, is based on pre-modern units of mobilisation. Most political parties rely on the well-worked units of caste, community, regional or linguistic groups for mobilisation of votes and for muscling in for space within the political process.

In 1971 Indira Gandhi had experimented with mobilisation over the head of these units with her slogan of '*garibi hatao*'. The overwhelming response to her appeal gave her a fright as much as to the Opposition parties; the experiment has never been repeated. We are thus back to the community, caste and so on as the operative units. Thus all the social and political tensions that any process of development generates are being directed into the communal channel by the ruling party as well as by most Opposition parties, resorting, of course to different strategies. Unlike in medieval centuries when conflict at the political level between two religious groups did not generate conflicts at the social level, today when political processes are essentially based on mass mobilisation, any attempt by any political party to participate in the political process with the mobilisation of one or more community or caste is bound to create fissures at the social level. True that this mobilisation allows the mass of Indian people a share, however meagre, in the politial process. But the very success of such mobilisation reinforces the communal, the caste, the regional and the linguistic identities, making the subsequent intervention of these groups in the political process even more aggressive. The all-round aggressive intervention of communal forces is today far more marked than it was during the preceding decades and there is little likelihood of its subsidence. For the very process of India's economic and political modernisation has lent enormous vitality to these 'traditional' forces.

Class category

The true alternative to communalism then is not the "specific Indian notion of secularism" but a polity based on an operative category that stands alone and in opposition to the category of community, caste and the like—the category of class. This category is not coterminous with but inclusive of economic analysis; it also includes cultural and philosophical perceptions. If the Left parties, professing to work with the category of class, have often made compromises with communal courses under the compulsions of parliamentary democracy, they are also capable of getting out of these compromises, for 'community' is not central to their thinking as it is to that of the non-Left parties. But the polity based on the concept of class is an alternative to the present-day polity in its totality, and not merely in those parts that relate to the question of communalism. And that is a good enough reason why the dominant elements in our polity will not allow the alternative to establish itself; it would rather that communal tensions than class tensions prevailed.

Ayodhya Dispute
Tool for Political Mobilisation

The Hindu, 1.11.1990

For the discipline of history three kinds of evidence are of vital significance; archaeology, written texts and inscriptions, and popular tradition. It should therefore be fair to examine the status of the Ram Janambhoomi-Babri Masjid dispute in terms of the historiccl evidence derived from these sources.

That Rama was a mythological, rather than a historical, figure is hardly a matter of dispute; it is possible, however, that some or many, of the characters portrayed in the Ramayana did actually exist and some of the events described there did actually take place, though their scale and historical significance may have differed from the one mythology came to attach to them at some stage. For argument we shall assume Rama to be a historical figure.

The first epic woven around the story of Rama is of course the Ramayana of Valmiki. According to this text, Rama, king of Ayodhya, was born in the Treta Yuga, that is several thousand years before the Kali Yuga which began in 3102 B.C. However, the archaeological excavations, undertaken by the former Director-General of the Archaeological Survey of India, Professor B.B. Lal, have established that there is no evidence of any kind of habitation in modern-day Ayodhya before the eighth century B.C. when the first signs of settlement of a rudimentary nature appear. This is in sharp contrast to the highly sophisticated urban setting against which the events described in the Ramayana are supposed to have taken place. Clearly then Valmiki could not have had this Ayodhya in mind where Rama was born.

Indeed it is not even clear where the Ayodhya of Rama is located, for several texts place it on the banks of the river Ganga rather than Saryu where the present one stands. Against this extremely uncertain background the claim of absolute certainty of the exact place of Rama's birth appears more than a little suspect.

Babur mosque

It is possible of course that popular tradition has for long established the particular spot where Babur is said to have built his mosque as Rama's birthplace and where a temple is supposed to have been erected(though when and by whom this was done is entirely unknown). I shall return to the question of this tradition later.

Meanwhile let us look at the evidence about the construction of the mosque at the site of the temple. The structure known as Babari mosque was built by Mir Baqi, a noble of the Mughal emperor, on the latter's express instruction. This is known from the Persian verses inscribed on the inner as well as the outer faces of the mosque door. The verses, however, merely state that Mir Baqi had built the mosque but do not refer to the destruction of any temple nor to any sanctity attached to that site by any group of people. Babur himself records in 1528 his visit to Ayodhya twice on the same page in his Memoirs and states that he undertook some administrative tasks there, but makes no mention of building the mosque, much less of the destruction of any temple.

Abul Fazl, courtier of Akbar and author of the great work, *Ain-i-Akbari*, refers to Ayodhya as the city where Rama was born but does not locate any site of his birth, nor does he record the destruction of a temple to make way for the mosque. Indeed no historical or any other work written in medieval India, often by fundamentalist Muslim authors, mentions the construction of this mosque at the site of a temple, and no imperial descendant of emperor Babur, not even the fanatic Aurangzeb—himself responsible for the destruction of several Hindu temples and construction of mosques at their site—makes any reference to it.

If this is surprising even more suprising is the absence of any mention of it in the works of Goswami Tulsi Das, author of the second great epic on the theme of Rama's life, the Ramacharitamanas. Tulsi Das was an inhabitant of Ayodhya and wrote the epic in his native Awadhi dialect. A lifelong devotion to Rama had given him a rare boldness, such that he curtly turned down an invitation by Emperor Akbar himself to visit the imperial court. If the temple built to commemorate Rama's own birth place at Ayodhya had indeed been demolished just 60 or 70 years before he was composing his epic, the memory of it would surely have driven him hopping mad. And yet, all we have from him is dead silence! Nor do we get any reference to it in any of the medieval historical or literary works, whether the author was Hindu or Muslim, orthodox or liberal.

It is only in the 19th century that the legend of the demolition of the temple and construction of the mosque begins to get into the records. In 1822 Hafizullah, an official of the Faizabad law-court submitted the following statement to the court : "The mosque founded by emperor Babur is situated at the birth place of Rama, son of Raja Dashrath, (and is) adjacent to the kitchen of Sita, wife of Rama." Indeed, during the 19th century there is a spurt in disputes over the issue and tradition seems to have grown that the mosque had displaced the temple. The story then gets into the records like P. Carnegy's historical sketch of Faizabad (1870), H.R. Nevill's Faizabad District Gazetteer, and as a foot note to Mrs. A.S. Beveridge's English translation of Babur's Memoirs (1922).

Clearly therefore the belief or tradition, which is today the basis of the VHP-BJP claim that a particular spot was the exact place of Rama's birth so many thousand years ago cannot be pushed beyond the 18th century at the most, after leaving a margin for the origin of the tradition and its incorporation into recorded history. The BJP is aware of this weakness and therefore refuses to summon history to its defence and would not abide even by the Supreme Court's judgment; its claim rests on what it seeks to represent as the 'belief' of millions of Hindus.

Incidentally there are at least a dozen temples at Ayodhya each claming to be the birth place of Rama and each adducing popular tradition for legitmising the claim. The Hindus of Ayodhya do not seem to think much of the VHP-BJP's self-confident assertions considering that their constituency has elected a CPI candidate who had made the falsity of this dispute his main issue in the last Lok Sabha elections.

Prayer together

Anyway, since the 19th century, despite occasional disputes, Hindus and Muslims had been saying their prayers at the open platform and the adjacent built-up mosque respectively. It was on December 22, 1949 at midnight that according to an FIR lodged by police Sub-inspector Ram Dube of the Ayodhya police station, a group of 50 or 60 persons entered the Babari mosque and established therein an idol of Shri Bhagwan and painted Sita Ram on the walls. Akshay Brahmachari, a Gandhian and secretary DCC, Ayodhya went on a hunger strike in protest. The gates to the temple and mosque were then locked by the Administration and the disputes lay dormant until Mr. Rajiv Gandhi had the locks opened in 1986 to balance the Muslim Women's Bill.

It would therefore appear that the BJP has latched itself on to an issue which had remained a non-issue ever since its origin at the most two centuries ago. In a way this too calls for some explanation, which I believe lies in the working of our polity.

Since Independence India has experimented with a very modern political system, namely parliamentary democracy based on universal adult franchise and multi-party elections. Its modernity can be appreciated from the fact that universal adult franchise came to the U.K. and the U.S. only in the 1930s, to Canada in 1940, to France in 1944 and to Switzerland in 1973 when women in these countries got the voting right; it came to India in 1950. And it is only now in the 1990s that the former socialist block is going in for multiparty elections. Yet this breathtakingly modern political process operates in India mostly with pre-modern units of mobilisation.

Nehru's vision

In the liberal, Nehruvian vision, the underlying assumption was that the very modernity of industialisation as an economic experience and of parliamentary democracy as a political process would gradually force a retreat on the backward consciousness of the Indian people generated and sustained by centuries of economic, political, educational backwardness. What has happened in real life is the contrary. The 'backward' or pre-modern units of mobilisation such as community, caste, regional and linguistic affinities have been put to use for working this very modern political system.

On the one hand, this form of mobilisation has helped draw those groups into the political process, which would otherwise have got left out or whose integration with the working of the polity would have been long delayed: the various minority groups, the women, the strata at the lower rungs of the socio-economic ladder; on the other, the very success of such mobilisation has tended to reinforce those very primordal identities which it had sought to erode. Thus the space for such identities in our political process has tended to grow with the passage of time.

The BJP, conscious of this is seeking to enlarge its own space by embarking upon the project of consolidating the largest of such constituencies, namely Hindus. In that context it is unimportant for it whether or not historical evidence supports the claim on Ram Janmabhoomi, so long as it serves as an instrument of mobilisation.

However, the working of our polity has also shown that given the choice between this form of mobilisation and the one based on secular economic and political issues, the illiterate but politically extremely astute Indian electorate has always overcome its primordial identities and voted for the secular choice; this happened in 1967, 1971, 1977 and to an extent in 1980. The BJP might be able to turn the Temple issue into an electorate vote bank only if the other parties fail to face it with a clear cut secular choice. That only the future can tell. But the people of India are capable of producing great surprises.

BJP's Hindutva Ploy Gets Limited Results

TOI, 26.6.1991

The most striking feature of the 1991 elections is the regional variation of each party's support-base. Though the Congress has enhanced its tally from the ninth Lok Sabha, the increase in its strength from Tamil Nadu, Haryana and Madhya Pradesh has been offset by its virtual elimination from Uttar Pradesh and Bihar. Though the Left Front has created history of sorts in West Bengal by romping home with a thumping majority for the fourth successive time, it has fared very badly in Kerala where, on all accounts, it appeared to have been doing rather well and was expecting a comfortable majority. The Janata Dal has lost many of its Lok Sabha seats, yet it has done creditably in Bihar and even Uttar Pradesh.

It is evident then that no slogan or party or combination of parties was able to move the electorate uniformly across the length and breadth of the country, and that the regional image of each party determined the voting behaviour.

Killer instinct

Paradoxical as it may seem in this hour of BJP's glory, this party appears to have lost out most. More than any other party, the BJP had sought to carve out one single, massive Hindu vote bank across the country through a no-holds barred campaign on the Ram Janmabhoomi issue. Almost every kind of resource was mobilised for this struggle carried out with the 'killer instinct', from the moderate Mr. L.K. Advani and Mr. A.B. Vajpayee to the vituperative

Sadhvi Rithambhara and Uma Bharati, from the enormous organisational acumen of the RSS to the VHP and the lumpen Bajrang Dal, not to speak of the thousands of *sadhus*.

This was clearly a do-or-die campaign with a far more sanguine expectation of forming the government than the normal overstatement of electoral rhetoric. Yet the results demonstrate not only the failure of such a pan-Indian vote bank to materialise, but the restriction of the appeal of the Ram Janmabhoomi issue, as a mode of political mobilisation, even in the Hindi belt mainly to Uttar Pradesh.

Indeed, virtually the entire Hindi belt outside that state has turned its back on this issue as a vote catcher for the BJP though perhaps not as a religious issue in its own right. It follows then that it is the specific Uttar Pradesh situation in the overall Indian context, that explains the electoral encashment of this issue by the BJP. Even in Uttar Pradesh it is not the Janata Dal, the original antagonist of the BJP in the mandir-Mandal dichotomy, that has paid the heaviest price but the Congress. In Bihar too it is the Congress that has lost out in the Mandal vs mandir contest.

What seems to have set the BJP on the course of upward mobility of its expectations and their realisation, predominantly in Uttar Pradesh, is its almost unwitting emergence as virtually the only opposition to the V.P. Singh regime.

The opposition acquired political legitimacy as the regime in general and Mr. V.P. Singh in particular began increasingly to be perceived as hiding the lacklustre performance and spinelessness vis-à-vis political rivals within the ruling party behind pettyfoggying clothed in high-sounding principles. The Congress was then lying so low as almost to have become politically invisible, the Left parties were going all out in support of the government. The announcement of Mandal by Mr. V.P. Singh was clever in that no party could publicly oppose it; nor did they. Yet if implemented, the BJP would be the one party losing the most ground. It was only when the BJP's home constituency, the urban middle and lower middle class, began to express its enormous, though unorganised anger at Mandalisation that the BJP woke up to the possibilities of channelising this anger by positing an alternative to it.

Indeed, the decision on the *rathyatra* came very late, towards late September and then hesitantly for even on October 20, at the height of the *yatra's* success, Mr. Advani showed willingness to suspend the agitation following the government's ordinance acquiring the disputed land and property at Ayodhya. Clearly he was unsure how much dividend could be derived from Ram. It is when Mr. V.P. Singh succumbed to the Shahi Imam's pressure and withdrew the ordinance within 24 hours that Mr. Advani was left with no choice but to press on with the temple issue. The withdrawal of BJP support to the government following Mr. Advani's arrest on October 22 set up the party firmly as the only functioning opposition which had brought down a government that was seen by the urban intelligentsia to have greatly exceeded its mandate.

This image as the opposition came into sharp focus when the roles of the government and its chief adversary were being played out at Ayodhya throughout October but particularly on October 30 and November 2. Uttar Pradesh had become the battleground for what was on both sides purely manipulative politics. In this battleground the Mulayam Singh Yadav government was perceived as having committed many excesses where a softer handling of the situation might have carried greater popular support. These perceptions were no doubt magnified many times over by a hostile press and by the propaganda machine at the command of the BJP-VHP-Bajrang Dal-sadhus combine who were in any case operating in an atmosphere receptive to the widest rumours.

Positive profile

It is in this context that the BJP has benefited most in Uttar Pradesh though it has parially gained elsewhere too as the only organised political opposition. Once again the electorate, and the antipathy of other parties have assigned this role to it, though it was hoping for a more positive profile; once again, it might benefit from this role as the new government addresses itself to awesome tasks on the basis of an indecisive verdict. But it seems evident that the strategy of creating a pan-Indian solidarity for electoral purposes has not worked and is unlikely to work as several commentators had warned before the elections.

Meanwhile, the Indian electorate, politically astute as ever has for the nth time sent out the the message that it will not be taken for granted on any count; caste, community, religion, political allegiance or whatever and that it prefers straight political alternatives to religous or caste identities while making political choices.

Time of Political Flux

The Pioneer, 15.4.1992

The temple issue is no longer valid

The signification of the recent happenings at Ayodhya has been analysed by the Press as a referrent that is internal and exclusive to the BJP. Even *The Pioneer MRAS/Burke* findings have been so analysed, for example, by Kanchan Gupta (*The Pioneer*, April 7). Illuminating as this analysis is, it nevertheless misses out on the greater importance of these happenings which perhaps lies in their being a pointer to the political scenario as a whole rather then merely as an attribute of the BJP.

If the BJP and the RSS *parivar* are keen to project the demolition of smaller temples and the acquisition of land, etc. as steps towards the fulfilment of their electoral pledge on the Ram temple issue, the absence of any semblance of popular euphoria over these steps could not possibly have been more deafening.

The contrast between the decisive BJP political intervention in the wake of Mr. L.K. Advani's *rath yatra* and the subsequent elections and the almost pathetic response to its initiatives on the same issue today, should caution us against the assumption that BJP owes its impressive electoral performance to the temple issue alone and that this issue remains its best electoral bet still.

The temple issue did not move up the political agenda of the country on its own; its upward movement was much more the handiwork of its role as crystallised opposition to the Mandal issue which the V.P. Singh Government had sought to foist upon the body politic and carve out political space for itself. This was the time when the Congress was a silent, almost indifferent, spectator to events taking shape independently of it and the Left parties, the traditional Opposition, were tailing the Janata Dal.

The Mandal issue has the advantage for the Janata Dal in that no political party, not even the BJP, could dare publicly oppose it, though it was the one to be most severely hit by the former's success. Nor indeed, did the BJP oppose it initially; it was only when the expression of hostility by students and the urban lower middle class constituency showed the direction of the political wind that the party woke up to the role of the Opposition.

It was this role, taking the form of Mandir vs Mandal that projected the BJP on to centrestage even though it played the role—at least initially—rather reluctantly, with Mr. Advani looking out for any compromise even two days before he was arrested at Samastipur at the height of his *rath yatra* glory.

Therefore there was never doubt in any one's mind that the BJP's commitment to building the temple would be reciprocal upon the electoral advantage and that the temple was the great vote mobiliser. The linkage was symbolised by the display of the lotus on Mr. Advani's *rath* and in his subsequent statement that he was a political, not a religious, leader.

Thus, the promise of a temple not only released enormous emotional energies of the people but served as a filler of the political vacuum that the growing failure of V.P. Singh's political strategy was creating. For the BJP to assume then that the issue would continue to play the same role for it, independently of the political context, would lend it an eternity, whereas all it possessed was a certain immediacy at a certain juncture. If the Mandal issue is dead, the Mandir issue cannot remain alive and kicking for long.

Indeed, it is in the nature of politics, or for that matter, social concerns in general that each mode and agenda of mobilisation is constantly displacing other modes and agendas, and is in turn being constantly contested by still others. Mrs. Indira Gandhi was experimenting with the Hindu card for the 1984 election when she was assassinated; her body gave a boost to that sentiment displacing the BJP by reducing it to a miserable two seats in the Lok Sabha out of the 222 it contested. Corruption and Bofors paid put to the Congress in 1989. The Mandal, and in opposition to it, Mandir issues set the agenda for the 1991 election. And since then, it is the economy that has occupied centrestage and no amount of mobilization on the Mandir issue will evoke any response in competition with the economic issues.

It is here that the BJP's, or for that matter, the entire political spectrum's dilemma lies. On one hand, the Mandir issue lies in a shambles, for, the first and the most important lesson in politics is that one cannot beat a political drum twice; on the other, the BJP, or other parties are finding it difficult to play any role as the Opposition with the economy at the top of the agenda; for virtually nothing of the old ideologically conditioned differences of perspectives on the economy survives.

The leftist and the rightist perspective have all merged into the centre. There is little that various parties, including the Congress, can offer to the electorate on this crucial issue that demarcates them from one another. The BJP believes it is obliged to keep the Ayodhya issue alive as its benchmark, even in the face of its receding appeal, for it has nothing else to go by.

The Left parties have lost out on the validation of their ideology on precisely the score that they had handed out as its sheet anchor, namely the efficacy of socialist regimes. But the Left will perhaps still survive in some regions and increasingly give up its nation-wide ambitions.

The Congress is having a good time for the moment, but then it has never needed an adversary to subvert it. Time of flux, if ever there was one.

Abode of the Angels?

The Pioneer 10.8.1992

Mir Baqi does not talk of a temple destroyed

The earliest evidence of the construction of the Babri Masjid is inscribed on the walls of the building itself in the form of two verses from three Persian couplets. It says:

In the name of One who is Omniscient
Creator of the Worlds, (but) Himself abodeless
In salutation to the Prophet, beyond all praise
The Chief among prophets of the two worlds
Narrating to the world the story of Babur the Recluse
Who has attained to the height of worldly success... and,
By the command of Emperor Babur whose justice
Is an edifice reaching up to the very height of the heavens
The goodhearted Mir Baqi
Built this alighting place of angels
May this goodness last forever!
The year of its construction becomes manifest in saying
May this goodness last forever

Thus, Mir Baqi expressly states that he was carrying out Babur's command in erecting the mosque, 'the alighting place of angels.' But the inscriptions do not in any way indicate that the mosque had been constructed at the site of an already existing structure, much less a temple of any sort; nor do they suggest that the place was invested with any sanctity by any set of people.

Babur himself records his visit to Ayodhya in 1528, twice on the same page of his Memoirs, and mentions his sundry doings, including a hunt. But he shows no recognition of a Ram temple and therefore, not surprisingly, records no order for its demolition and the construction of a mosque instead.

The next bit of evidence comes from *Ain-i Akbari* of Abul Fazl, compiled in 1595. Abul Fazl recognises Ram's association with Ayodhya, but does not locate any site of his birth, or a temple there, and makes no mention of Babri Masjid at all. He observes: "It was the residence of Ramchandra who in the Treta age combined in his own person both the spiritual supremacy and kingly office."

If Babur as emperor, and Abul Fazl as a historian, do not record the erection of the mosque at the site of a temple, they are not alone in their silence. None of Babur's imperial descendants, not even the bigoted Aurangzeb, who was responsible for the destruction of several temples and the construction of mosques in the place of some, including the ones at Mathura and Kashi, reminisce about the building of the Babri mosque at the site.

Nor do the string of historians, of various ideological hues, all members of the imperial court, make any mention whatsoever of the destruction of a sacred temple.

If this is surprising, even more surprising is the complete absence of the mention of it in the works of any of the Hindi poets, most of them Hindus. Among them was Goswami Tulsi Das, a resident of Ayodhya, who wrote his epic, *Ramcharitamanas* and other poems, in his native Awadhi. The epic was composed within five decades of the construction of the mosque, within the poet's living memory. Yet, all the we hear from him on this is dead silence.

Indeed, silence is all that we encounter in the imperial edicts, official histories and documents, literary works of all gerres, European travellers accounts...

The first clear, uncontestable evidence that the mosque was built at the site of Ram's birth is contained in a document submited to the Faizabad court by its superintendent, one Hafizullah, in 1238 H/1822 AD. Here is the translation: "The Jama Masjid, constructed by Emperor Babur is located at the

Janmasthan, that is, at the site of the birth of Ram, son of Raja Dasrat (and is) adjacent to the building of the Rasoi (kitchen) of Sita, wife of the above-mentioned Ram..."

The document leaves no one in doubt about the linkage between the mosque and Rama Janambhoomi; yet it does not mention any temple having existed at the site and that it had been demolished to make way for the mosque.

In the 19th century, things moved fast and a Ram temple had found location in some versions of the dispute, of which there were several. But it was still shaky in the 1860s to have prompted P. Carnegy conjecturing about the existence of a temple at the site, building his theory on the black stone pillars embedded in the mosque, but still not quite sure whether the temple was dedicated to Ram or to Buddha.

Mandir or Masjid?

The Pioneer, 11.8.1992

The temple theory is based on oral history

In the 19th century, P. Carnegy put it on record that a Babri mosque had indeed displaced the earlier Ram temple and professedly bases his statement on 'locally affirmed' information, that is, popular tradition.

By 1905, the story had made its way to the *Gazetteer* of Faizabad district. Mrs. A. Beveridge, translator of the *Babur Nama*, picked up the story from the *Gazetteer* and turned it into a definitive account of the destruction of a Ram temple and the construction of Babri Masjid in its place. All she needed to do was make an assumption that Babur, by virtue of being a Muslim, must have been intolerant of all other religions and would have considered it his pious duty to convert a Hindu shrine into a mosque.

The demolition of the Ram temple and the construction of the Babri Masjid, then, is an inference drawn from the fact of Babur being a Muslim.

While the Muslim rulers of medieval India comprised a wide spectrum with an enormous variation in their disposition, Babur was not particularly renowned for his religious zeal or iconoclasm.

Indeed, on his visit to Gwalior in September 1529, while he ordered the destruction of some erotic sculptures as he was aghast at the display, he made it a point to visit other 'idol-houses' of the town and reports 'enjoying the sight of these building'.

At any rate, if one were to follow the train of Mrs. Beveridge's logic that being a Muslim meant being a destroyer of places of worship belonging to other religions, one would expect Babur to proclaim the demolition of the Ram temple and the construction of the mosque with great hyperbole, considering the antiquity and the dignity of the site, as she puts it.

His silence and that of everyone else, on whichever side of the fence, until as late as the first quarter of the 19th century, therefore, does much damage to Mrs. Beveridge's logic.

It should be reasonable to argue that the entry of the story into a legal document of 1822 would point to a pre-history. There is, indeed, a strong popular tradition in the region that the Babri Masjid stands at the site of Ram's birth and that it has displaced a temple dedicated to him. The historian must give popular tradition due respect as a piece of evidence of another genre compared with documented proof.

But popular tradition could either be a historian's subject of study as a cultural phenomenon evolving over long periods of time, or else, it must be rigorously historicised if it is to serve as evidence for a particular historical event.

To insist on popular tradition as proof of the existence and demolition of a Ram temple and the construction of the Babri Masjid in a particular year is to misconstrue the nature of tradition since the notion of time in popular tradition is never so precise as it is in history.

Going by the 1822 record, it would, therefore, appear that the story of the Masjid standing at the site of Ram's birth had started growing sometime earlier, perhaps in the 18th century, and somewhere during the 19th century the site also came to be associated with a Ram temple.

It would be extremely interesting to trace the evolution of this tradition in the social, political and psychological fabric and in the setting of religious beliefs. But it is still poor evidence for an event which had taken place anywhere between two and three centuries earlier.

The black stone pillars embedded in the existing structure

are still to be contended with. P. Carnegy noticed these pillars in the 1860s and sought to conjecture the existence of a temple. If Carnegy was not certain whether the carved pillars suggested a Ram or a Buddhist temple, no such doubt assails the VHP.

According to the VHP, the pillars supported an existing structure of a Ram temple; they were therefore *in situ*. However, right at the entrance to the building which encloses the courtyard, two such pillars form part of the wall and the carving on them is completely different from each other. Of the 14 pillars that have been used in the walls, the carving on 10 is dissimilar and there is no order in which they have been placed. It is clear then that the pillars could not possibly have been *in situ*, that they had been brought over from somewhere else.

Evidence from medieval history of virtually any genre would thus cast serious doubts on the VHP's claim.

What Do We Tell Firozi Then?

The Pioneer, 1.9.1993

Firozi is our current domestic help. She needed the quarter attached to the house rather badly but did not want to show it; we needed help badly too but were equally circumspect about letting her know. The negotiations went round the whole gamut of the chores, the salary, etc. before moving on to her family.

Her husband was a peon in a 'private big company' was all she knew of his official existence. What was his name? "Name?" she repeated, incredulous at the audacity of the question, "I don't know."

It gradually dawned on us that that we were committing a sacrilege by asking a devout Indian wife to pronounce her husband's name. But she was willing to throw hints. He was she said, a *das* of the Rasool. Through several tries we finally arrived at Ghulam Muhammad and she coyly nodded her approval.

On the number of children in her family, the ambiguity of her answer would have delighted a hardened post-modernist: about, like three or four, she said. As she moved in, we realised that beneath the ambiguity lay a solid rock of objective facts: her brood counted seven heads, all told.

The eldest is a girl, Anju; the next is a son, Imtiaz. The third is a darkish-skinned lad bestowed with the rather unfelicitous name Kaloo, a delightful bundle of childish pranks. The others are yet too young to acquire identities of their own. But the house remains surprisingly quiet even with all of them around.

Firozi herself would rather be seen dead than without a red bindi on her forehead and sindur running through half of her scalp, renewed every morning. Bindi alright, but sindur in the parting of a Muslim woman's hair? That made us a bit curious but we did not know how to ask.

So we resorted to the tested techniques of seminars—asking a leading question. Since when has she been using sindur, we inquired. "Ever since the day I got married," she replied without demurring a moment. "How else could a woman indicate her marital status as well as hope for a long life for her husband?"

She had missed the import of our question. So the lady of the house tried again: was it herself who had decided on wearing the sindur? "No, no," she said vehemently, aghast at the appalling ignorance of the city bred, "every girl in our village in Bihar wears it on getting married."

"How can a marriage be sanctified without the sindur in the girl's hair?" she added with a touch of finality.

Since this line of enquiry was not yielding results, another tack was tried: "What are the festivals you celebrate?"

"Didi," she replied with a trace of despondency, "what festivals can we poor people celebrate? Festivals are meant for those with a lot of money."

"Even so," the LOH, steeped in the methodology of social science research, was not going to give up easily, "there must be some festivals in the year you would celebrate. Like Id, for example."

"Yes, Didi," she conceded, "there is Id and there is Holi and Diwali. Of these, Diwali is the most beautiful." It became difficult to hold her back from interminably recounting the beauty of her village when every household was lit up with lamps on Diwali night.

A dreadful thought strikes me as I write these lines: What if some day this family gets caught up in the whirpool of communal frenzy and its tormentors announce triumphantly that another group of people had been made to pay the price of not belonging to the national mainsteam. Shall we be able to look Firozi or Ghulam Muhammad or Anju in the eye?

Tide is Turning on Vote Bank Theory

TOI, 15.6.1995

Maulana Wahiduddin Khan has, in his 'Muslim Leadership Has Failed Them' (May 17), opened up a debate that was long overdue. However, the complexity of the problem is somewhat diluted if it is considered with Muslims as its sole referrent. Any number of referrents intersect one another in the formation of a complex issue such as that of the Indian Muslims.

Both before and since Independence, the politically operative category has been the community. It is in terms of the community that both the Congress and the Muslim League analysed Indian society and mobilised the masses in the freedom struggle. If the League projected the impending decimation of the Muslims, should the Congress inherit power from the British, the Congress sought to reassure them of the security of their religious identity, above everything else, if they moved under its banner. The Congress sought to blend the communal identity of the Muslims with nationalism. The appeal of the Congress did not thus constitute an alternative to the League's; at best it was just half a step ahead. As such its power was always ephemeral: the first sign of communal tension, engineered by either side, would send the Muslims reeling into the League's fold. Even as empirically the League and the Congress were each other's negation, conceptually operating with the same analytical category, i.e., the community, the two comprised a continuum in which their positions and tactics often became interchangeable.

Same category

Since Independence, the same category of the community has been operative in the working of the very modern Indian political process, i.e., parliamentary democracy. Its modernity notwithstanding, the units of mobilisation have been the community, caste, etc., encapsulated in the evocative term 'vote bank'. Each political party has sought to constitute its vote bank in terms of a combination of castes, communities, etc. culminating in the BJP's attempt to constitute the biggest vote bank of all, i.e. the Hindus, chiefly with reference to what it projected as the 'other', i.e. the Muslims. A major assumption of this attempt was the possibility of marginalisation of the Muslims in the working of the electoral process and undermining the bases of Congress support. Legitimacy to the attempt was imparted by the Congress' surrender to the strident call of the Muslim leadership on the Shah Bano case.

However, as the working of parliamentary democracy unfolds, many of the assumptions of virtually all political parties are being belied. The BJP's attempt to constitute the Hindu solidarity led to the demolition of the Babri Masjid and the subsequent defeat in the state of U.P. and elsewhere. Equally important, the assumption that was widely shared then that the Muslims being in a sullen mood would turn insular and withdraw from the parliamentary politics which had led to this assault on their very identity was firmly repudiated and the Muslims voted en masse and contributed to the defeat of the BJP. They thus owned the electoral process as a democratic means in which they could change things. Similarly, their contribution to the defeat of the Congress in Maharashtra and Gujarat is well known. More significantly, the dead silence that has followed the Supreme Court's recent directive to the government regarding a uniform civil code is almost deafening in comparison with the very noisy intervention of the Muslim leadership following the far more innocuous Shah Bano judgement. The community's silence also in the aftermath of the burning down of Charar-e-Sharief is voluble. And now the news of Mr. A.K. Antony's victory from a predominantly Muslim constituency! What has changed the scenario of the Indian Muslims?

Two results

I believe as the power of the vote as the agency of change within the given structure is realised, two consequences are surfacing: on one hand, history, especially the brief but climactic history of pre-Independence India is receding into the background, even though Maulana Wahiduddin takes us back precisely there; and, on the other, the stereotypes of electoral behaviour, never completely valid anyway, are getting further eroded. The 'vote bank' stereotype is the chief among them and this concerns not the Muslims alone but all vote banks. In other words, religious frenzy as the chief mobiliser of political and electoral support has begun to yield diminishing returns. If silence from the Muslim community has greeted the Supreme Court's directive on the civil code, the arrest of that incomparable rabble-rouser, Ms Sadhavi Ritambhara, with not a whiff of a stirring being heard anywhere, too is indicative of the direction of the flow of the wind. The hope then lies in this profound, though subtle change, in the public gaze being fixed at the future rather than the past.

BJP Remoulds Itself

The Pioneer, 14.7.1995

Hazardous as it is to predict the pattern of electoral behaviour of the politically astute Indian voter, the straws in the wind do seem to point to a possible victory of the BJP in the parliamentary elections due in 1996. This is not on account of the BJP's innate strength, but more by default of the Congress and the Government.

The spectacular rise of the BJP from a dismal two seats in the Lok Sabha to 88 in 1989 elections owed itself to a complex scenario, but one of the major contributions was from the Rajiv Gandhi Government which made a quick surrender to the dogmatic but vociferous Muslim leadership on the issue of Shah Bano in overruling the Supreme Court judgement.

This gave legitimacy to the BJP charge that the Congress government was pampering the minorities. If, however, the BJP had hoped to romp home in a triumphant march after the demolition of the Babri Masjid and the ensuing communal violence, the voter gave it some lesson in humility in Uttar Pradesh, Madhya Pradesh, and elsewhere.

One lesson that the BJP does appear to have learnt well is that between bringing issues to the brink and actually crossing it, political costs can rise very high. Therefore, ever since the riots of Bombay in the first week of January 1993, there have been no more significant communal riots anywhere and the BJP has re-crossed the river from losing governments to winning them again, without giving up its Hindutva plank. In the process, it also seems to be on the way to ending its isolation from other, even self-professed secular parties, such as George Fernandes' Samata Party.

Once again a scenario most favourable to the disposition of the BJP appears to be emerging. When the Allahabad High Court decided some time ago that the practice of triple *talaq* among Muslims would not do and therefore the civil code called for a second look, the judgement was greeted by an eloquent silence from the Muslim community, itself in turmoil after the failure of its traditional leadership on virtually all fronts. But the Narasimha Rao Government sat inert.

More recently the Supreme Court's intervention on the question of a common civil code was again met by a dead silence on the part of the leadership of the Muslim community, as was the arrest of Sadhvi Ritambhara by the Hindus, inspite of the BJP-VHP's attempts to stoke some fire.

Here was a pointer that the Indian society as a whole would rather forget the past and look to the future. Clearly the earlier operative equation that the urge for reform in the Muslim community must come from within the community was getting quietly eroded, for, essentially it put a premium on stasis within the community and therefore thwarted any challenge to its traditional leadership.

But the Narasimha Rao Government, true to form, sat smiling, like the Buddha. This smile of inertia has sent out the message that the old equation is still a functioning one, a little noise here and there notwithstanding. Understandably then, the noises have begun to emerge from quarters within the Muslim community that had been put on the defensive from within.

Nothing helps the BJP more than the image of a monolithic, backward, unchanging Muslim community, mired in the past and steeped in dogmatic moorings, 'the other' of the Hindu community; conversely, nothing erodes its appeal as much as a dynamic, forward-looking Muslim community struggling to come to terms with the imperatives of modern life.

That latter image had begun to emerge paradoxically

since the demolition of the Babri Masjid when the failure of the traditional leadership had become all too evident.The evidence of it was in the decisive participation of the Muslims in the electoral process since that fateful day at Ayodhya, making their own choices and refusing to get dictated to by traditional loyalties or leadership, combined with the silence on the judgments which concern the civil code.

But then silences in politics can be as decisive as loud proclamations. The silence of the Government to move an inch on the directives of the Courts have let the old leadership of the community know that it need not remain on the defensive any more and the old game can be played over again.

Clearly, the BJP is going to make this a major electoral plank in 1996. If any government, State or Central, announces reservation of jobs for Muslims, irrespective of its percentages, the BJP would find the field cut and dried for it. Without any need for unleashing violence, it would be able to consolidate the Hindutva plank and win an electoral victory. Whether or not it will feel grateful to Mr. Narasimha Rao and Mr. Sita Ram Kesari is another matter.

Muslims in Silent Secular Ferment

TOI, 22.1.1996

If one phrase could capture the mind of the Indian Muslims since Independence, it would perhaps be 'siege mentality'. Almost everyone concerned with the Muslim community contributed to this mentality. The orthodox Muslim leadership symbolised today in Imam Bukhari and Syed Shahabuddin, reveled in projecting the image of the community as if it were on the brink of collapse. The liberal Muslim intelligentsia reinforced the 'community in decline' picture by harping on the decline of Urdu and the under-representation of Muslims in government jobs. The Congress could feel secure about the Muslim vote by forever bringing home to the community the RSS sword hanging over its head. And the RSS and its family members could turn around the Congress' 'protection' to the Muslims as pampering them. The Left parties contested communalism, but they were frequently willing to underrate minority communalism and the problems it created for the Muslim community itself.

Main premise

The dominant premise of this scenario may be termed politics of visible symbols. Each group imaged the community either in decline or being overly favoured in terms of the number of heads in high-flying positions. The high degree of its stratification, like in the other communities, was consequently overlooked. Had that been taken into account, both the propositions of its uniform decline or universal pampering would have appeared as dubious. Like their other fellow

Indians, a small segment of the Muslims has done exceedingly well for itself since Independence, a large chunk lives below the poverty line and the largest portion lives in between.

'Pampering' too has brought affluence and recognition to an infinitesimal number of Muslim individuals and families, though, like with the other communities, not always well merited. If the Muslim percentage in government jobs does not square with its demographic strength, it does not by itself substantiate the image of the community in an economic crisis, for the economy's reach surely is immensely greater than government jobs. Nor indeed has Urdu suffered the kind of decline attributed to it. To take just one example, the number of Urdu newspapers and journals in 1958 was 185; in 1990 it had risen to 2,003. Their circulation too had risen from 4.4 lakh to 25.4 lakh. In both years the Urdu papers were next only to those of Hindi and English in numbers and in circulation.

The twin image of decline and pampering are two sides of the same coin, though with an in-built tension. It was this tension which led to the demolition of the Babri Masjid at Ayodhya on December 6, 1992. In the immediate aftermath of December 6 what was most feared was the withdrawal of the Muslims into insular shells in sullen mood. What really has happened is the contrary: the community at large is, in a silent ferment, challenging the dichotomy itself, its massive participation in the elections in the wake of the Ayodhya event, and owning up the political process through which it could change governments, is one manifestation of its response.

In the late 1940s and early 1950s in the context of the country's partition along communal divide, many Muslims who rose high in India did so by virtually erasing their religious identity publicly. Thus Dilip Kumar, Meena Kumari and Madhubala had to erase their Muslim names and adopt those of the Hindus to find acceptances as film actors and actresses. Today Shahrukh Khan and Aamir Khan wouldn't think of sacrificing their names and their Muslim identity at the altar of success. A similar change is noticeable even at the lower rungs of society. The number of scooter rickshaws flaunting *khuda hafiz* or the number 786 (spiritual symbol of Islam) recently in Delhi is impressive.

This sea change seems to have impressed Ms Sameen Khan, a Pakistani visitor who writes in 'Proud to be an Indian' in the *Nation and the World*: "I was impressed by the spirit of nationalism among the Indian Muslims and I felt envious and wished we in Pakistan would learn a lesson from it." After interacting with a cross-section of the Muslim community in Bombay, she also found the Muslims better off economically than on her previous visit eight years earlier.

Breaking shell

The mass of Muslims is thus quietly breaking out of the strait-jacket in which the working of Indian polity over the past nearly five decades had tied them. They have shown a definitive will to face modern life's challenges as they come, instead of brooding over the issues of the masjid and the triple *talaq*. In doing so they erode not merely the leadership of their own community which had thrived on constructing the fear of ever impending doom; they are also rewriting the digits of indirect politics, including BJP's politics. For, the BJP, above all, needs to besiege the Muslim community for Hindu vote bank. Not finding the Muslim response to its satisfaction, the BJP is constantly on the lookout for alternative forms of mobilisation.

Indeed, the whole spectrum of the Indian political scene has repeatedly given out signals that it wished to look to the future rather than the past. Repeatedly the *sangh pariwar* as well as the BMAC- type leadership have failed to mobilise support for religio-political issues in recent times. It is after all not insignificant that the events of December 6 and the devastating communal riots that followed in its wake also showed the limits to which communal tension could be driven. Since then there has mercifully been quiet on this front, what with large number of elections to state assemblies having taken place peacefully.

Cautious Optimism on Communal Politics

TOI, 23.10.1996

An interesting paradox seems to have marked the political scene over the past few years: a steady rise in the electoral acceptability of the Bharatiya Janata Party, invariably characterised as the archetypal communal outfit by its adversaries; and the absence of any major communal riot since the dastardly violence unleashed in the wake of the demolition of the Babri Masjid in December 1992. Compared to the fact that rarely had a year passed without the occurrence of a few hundred riots being reported to parliament by the Home Ministry in the preceding two decades, these four years appear remarkably reassuring.

Can we then hope to see the end of the politics of communal riots?

BJP's strategy

Understandably, several streams have contributed to the emerging denouement. The BJP's own extremist Hindutva project has got diluted as its space in the political mainstream expanded. Its strategy of forging a uniform identity of the Hindus had a degree of egalitarian appeal in it inasmuch as it sought to blur the sectarian and caste dividing lines under the single colour of the saffron banner. But the reality of caste identities forced a two-fold dilution. On the one hand, the upper caste core of its ideology as well as resistance from the upper caste supporters for pragmatic political considerations moderated the implementation of the strategy; on the other hand, the growing Dalit support for the BJP too generated its own increasingly aggressive refusal to be taken for granted without commensurate space within the BJP spectrum. This phenomenon is best symbolised in the virtual indispensability of Mr. Kalyan Singh as the BJP's projected chief minister in U.P. The tensions within the BJP point to both its political dynamism and insecurities regarding its strategic ambitions.

There is also the counting of costs of communal riots—economic dislocation, political instability and cultural consequences of fractured inter-community ties. These seem to have been the chief lessons from the last bout of riots in December 1992 and the first half of January 1993. And the lessons have not been lost.

Not least has been the contribution of the silent, and therefore decisive, withdrawl of the Muslim community from the siege mentality that had been stoked by virtually every political grouping: the Congress, BJP, the orthodox as well liberal leadership of the Muslim community and indirectly, by the Left parties. All of them, except the BJP inverted the image by focusing on 'minorityism' in search of an aggressive articulation of a majority's solidarity. The result was the same—aggressive Hindutva reinforcing Muslim defensiveness.

But then, the Muslim community seems to have responded to the challenge in two ways: on the one hand it forced its old leadership to tone down any aggressive projection of the threat to its existence and on the other to explore alternative categories of self-assertion. One has only to compare the cacophony in the wake of the Shah Bano case with the virtual silence of orthodox Muslim leadership even after the demolition of the Babri Masjid and on other issues in many ways similar to the Shah Bano judgment.

Secular education

The increasingly voluble opinion within the community that

the way to survival and prosperity is in modern secular education and in self-help rather than in self-pity and blaming others goes hand-in-hand with the movement away from the half-century-old genre of Muslim politics. It is not insignificant that one no longer hears even the BJP haranguing the Muslims to be Indians first and Muslims second. The dichotomy embedded in being Indian-Muslim, whether articulated by the Hindutva forces or by leaders like Syed Shahabuddin has perhaps been rejected in favour of being both Indian and Muslim without any structured prioritisation.

The absence of Muslim aggression moderates the aggression of Hindu solidarity. It is not easy to sustain one-sided communal hysteria of which communal riots are an extreme manifestation. The era of politics without communal riots may not be very far.

The Artist and The Ideologue

The Pioneer, 18.10.1996

If the crime of burning down Husain's paintings by a gang of Bajrang Dal was heinous, Mr. K.R. Malkani's virtual justification of it is far worse. It attests to the continuum between a sweetly, even humorously written letter to the Editor (*The Pioneer,* October 11) and sheer vandalism in action. The mindset is common. What is the mindset?

Down to its essentials, the mindset is that every human being who has ever borne a Muslim name must for ever remain on trial before a jury that is also the accuser. Indeed, the trial is not on merely for Muslim individuals amidst us, but history itself, if associated with a Muslim, must account for whatever (and at whichever point in time) may in the eye of the accuser-jury constitute an injury to his body, mind and above all sentiment and must be made to pay for it.

From Mahmud of Ghazni, to Babur, Aurangzeb and now Husain there is only one identity and one motivation possible: the Msslim identity and Islamic zeal as their driving force. Not all the sophistication of historical explanation in terms of multiple motivations, not all the complexities of a human being's psychological make-up, not all the beauty of the formation and evolution of one's sensibilities through a grand cultural flux can balance the one single fact of being a Muslim.

The mindset is that once one is a Muslim, he is a Muslim —what else need be said about him? Husain in some ways epitomises the ideal always set before Indian Muslims by Mr. Malkani's party, the BJP, that the Indian Muslims must take pride in and identify themselves with Indian (i.e. Hindu) culture and religion.

Whenever Husain drew inspiration from a mythology for his art, which has been frequent, it was Hindu mythology. Whenever he painted any figure from a religious stream, it was the figures of Ganesha, Durga, Saraswati.

So immersed is he in this religio-cultural stream and so definitive is his own identification with it and of it with the essence of Indianness, that there is never a trace of selfconsciousness of a Muslim artist's representation of Hindu mythological figures in these paintings.

Clearly, the grandeur and aesthetics of this mythology have moved him as no other mythology has done, for a whole lifetime of great artistic creativity.

In this creativity Husain is also drawing upon the wellsprings of Indian social and cultural life where the village artist, Muslim by birth and a practising Muslim in many aspects of social and religious life, still draws and paints Durga and Kali, Radha and Krishna, to give expression to his or her inner urges without any conscious effort at 'national integration'; where a married Muslim girl would consider it sacrilegious to be seen without a hefty dose of sindur in the parting of her hair; where Hindu men would consider it unthinkable to start a new venture or set out on a long journey without seeking the blessings of the local pir, alive or long dead.

For these Indians the dividing lines between Hindu and Muslim religion and culture are not as sharp and clear as they are for the BJP and Mr. Malkani.

It is the tremendous energy and vitality of this cultural ambiguity at the folk-level that Husain is able to sublimate in his art. The spontaneity, the absence of deliberate interposition of his own religious identity one way or the other in his paintings of this genre is its most endearing feature.

But for all that he clearly cannot be forgiven by the Bajrang Dal and Mr. Malkani for bearing a Muslim name, which in their eyes becomes the unitary definition of his being. All complexities, ambiguities, subtleties dissolve before the stark clarity of his bearing a Muslim name.

Mr. Malkani does, however, prescribe a step to Husain to redeem himself if only in part: paint women from Muslim mythology and religious history in the nude and be quits.

For Mr. Malkani the politician, artistic creativity appears very similar to the formation of a cabinet—a good cabinet would balance regional, religious, caste and gender representation; a good artist would be one who paints figures in the same format from all mythologies, never mind all the nonsense about the artist's cultural ambience, inspiration, sensibilities, moods, whatever!

It is this ambiguity of Indianness, which amalgamates drops from different religious and cultural streams, that haunts Mr. Malkani's and his party's search for a clearcut Hindutva, for which a clearcut demonic Islam is an essential requisite, as a grand vehicle for that elusive smooth ride to power.

The price paid by the nation for the unfolding of this mindset in Kashmir, Punjab and generally in the aftermath of the demolition of the Babri Masjid has still not struck the Sangh parivar and Mr. Malkani as unaffordable, even as this vehicle to power is getting more and more rickety.

Demolishing Temples wasn't the Past's Only Language

The Hindustan Times, 19.3.2000

If we have increasingly to live with the wrapping of political nuances around the discipline of history, it is also important to recognise that this is by no chance either a very recent phenomenon or confined to the Indian landscape. All history writing—or, for that matter, all forms of knowledge —has been a discourse, an intervention in shaping society, the state, or the world, according to one given vision or another. History has thus forever been viewed as a clash of civilisations, of religions, of nations, of classes... .

History as 'science', as the unfolding of an objective truth through incremental scientific knowledge itself is one such discourse, growing out of strong Positivist roots, which in turn firmly places it in European context in the 19th and 20th centuries. Implicated in this discourse is European dominance of intellectual creativity around the world inasmuch as this vision spread out from Europe to the rest of the world during the two centuries in the wake of trade, arms and conquest.

The tradition of looking at history in India in terms of conflict of religions and sects goes back to hoary days: within the fold of the Hindu religion, between the Vaishnavites and the Saivites; between the Hindus and the Jainas and the Buddhists; between Brahminical Hinduism and ethnic groups, derisively referred to as the *dasyus*, and so forth.

In India's medieval centuries, one important construction

of history was in terms of conflict between Islam and *kufr*. The innumerable instances of the demolition of Buddhist *viharas* by Hindu rulers, in some cases of Hindu temples by Hindu rulers themselvs even within their own territory, of temples by Muslim rulers, of mosques by some local level Hindu rulers—all these, on one hand, reflect the assertion of state power by the rulers in the form of their religious identity, and on the other, their search for legitimisation in a vision of history.

As a people with history, therefore, we should not be taken by surprise at instances of this nature in any part of our remote past, for this was its language. The problem, however, arises from our assumption that this was the past's only language, that the state did nothing else except demolish temples and subjugate people of other faiths to its own, that historians never viewed history except as interminable religious clashes organised by the state. It is thus that just about any testimony, textual or archaeological, bearing upon history is immediately constructed as a proof of the state's religious intolerance.

Some two months ago, I got a call from a young reproter from *The Indian Express*, seeking my opinion on the excavations underway at Sikri and whether these attested to the demolition of Jaina temples by the Mughal emperor Akbar, who was building his palace fortress at Fatehpur Sikri. When I expressed my ignorance of the excavations and my inability to comment on the suggestion of demolition of temples unless I had seen the evidence for myself, she told me very excitedly of the unearthing of several Jaina statues and an exquisite Saraswati, all excavated from a small walled site which looked like having been a temple.

The news of the excavations excited many of us enough to organise a trip of three busloads of students and faculty, including teachers from colleges who were doing a refresher course at JNU to the site some two weeks ago. With generous help from the Archaeological Survey of India, we spent several hours at the site of excavation and the ASI guesthouse at Fatehpur Sikri, where the excavated statues have been stored.

We discussed with the two excavators, a young lady and a young gentleman, all aspects of the work going on. Both repeatedly emphasised, in a tone of caution that did credit to them and their profession, that the excavations had as yet yielded no definitive data and pointed to no certain conclusion.

The parts of walls still intact do not suggest any particular structure: either a temple or a house or any other. In fact, when they were asked whether it could just have been a dumping ground, they did not rule it out either. They were unwilling to commit themselves to any conclusion, even a suggestive one, until they had dug deeper. Quite fair, one would say.

The mound that is under excavation is known in the village around as Bir Chhabili's mound. Clearly it has no religious association. Bir Chhabili also does not seem to be a proper name, but more like a pet name, or one which expresses the lady's attributes and points to a young woman who was perhaps both romantic and audacious. Little else is known about the site in popular lore. Yet, it does seem to suggest a promising area for exploration. The region around this place is not a Jaina stronghold; there has therefore to be some extraordinary reason for establishing a Jaina temple there, and the present state of evidence does not shed any light on it.

At the excavated site, the legs of Mahavira in a meditative lotus position are still embedded in a part of the wall and there is no clear purpose of its location. Some other similar pieces have been stored in the guesthouse. There are also several torsos of Mahavira, clearly identificable because of the flower motif on his chest, and some heads.

The most exquisite of the sculptures there is the Jaina Saraswati, in seductive posture, with the face strongly resembling that of Mahavira. The sculpture is almost intact, with one hand broken off, but lying by its side. This gem of a sculpture was found lying face down at the mound about two metres from the surface. It had been as if placed there with reverence. This is the only piece virtually undamaged, except for the broken hand; all others bear several marks of deliberate or indeliberate vandalism.

Therefore, a suspicion: Is it feasible to consider the possibility of Brahminical intolerance, which spared the one goddess with clear Brahminical association, but not others which were, as it were, on the other side of the fence, that is, Jainism?

Remember, the possibility of the mound being a dumping ground had not been dismissed by the excavators: you dump the Saraswati there too for its Jaina associations, but show it due respect.

Of course, all this is pure speculation at this stage, as good or as bad as any other, and each as legitimate as the others, until evidence that is more conclusive comes forth.

That is not the problem. The problem is that any other speculation is disallowed, because the newspapers have decided that no other story, except one of Muslim demolition of non-Muslim temples will sell, and a former professor of physics and a former journalist have let it be known from their ministerial platforms that this is the only correct version of Indian history.

The digging under Fatehpur Sikri's Anup Talao, has just about begun (it had not, when we were around, two weeks ago), and already pronouncements have been made that it too hides a temple underneath!

Words of Wisdom!

The Hindu, 5.10.2002

It is very seldom that K.S. Sudarshan, Sarsanghchalak of the Rashtriya Swayamsevak Sangh (RSS), in any public utterance fails to lambast the Indian Muslims for being bullies (and correspondingly the Hindus for being cowards) or for refusing to own up the ancient Hindu mythological figures such as Ram and Krishna. Nor does he fail to cite the example of Indonesian Muslims in contrast who actually own up the figure of Ram in their land, and not being the worse for it. In his much-awaited public address to Delhi's 'inteligentsia' on Mahatma Gandhi's birthday, he repeated these gems of wisdom, as expected. These seem to constitute the limits of his knowledge about Islam and Hinduism. The other highlight of his address as reported in the press was staunch hostility to Western forms of economy. Knowledge, culture, even means of achieving hygiene for which we Indians are, he assured us, much better equipped thanks to the almost unlimited availability of cow's urine.

One assumes that Mr. Sudarshan finds all the learning that the RSS in its *shakhas* imparts for the complete education of an Indian, especially a Hindu, adequate. Those of us Indians, including Hindus, who did not have the benefit of getting educated in the *shakhas,* but elsewhere in schools and colleges, will feel rather disturbed on two counts. One, the grouping together of all Muslims and all Hindus under single heads is actually the legacy of western intellectual endeavour from the 18th century onward and in particular of the British colonial regime in India. The RSS has entirely and unquestioningly imbibed all of this and keeps diffusing in its *shakhas* and in such momentous public addresses as Mr. Sudarshan gave on October 2 and is likely to repeat on several other occasions.

Second, his assumption that the Indian Muslims withdraw themselves from any identification with Hindu religious or cultural symbols is derived from his probably brief and limited acquaintance with his own counterparts among the Muslims—persons such as Imam Bukhari or Syed Shahabuddin. Just as Mr. Sudarshan projects himself and persons such as Ashok Singhal and Praveen Togadia as the exclusive representatives of the Hindu community, religion and culture, he also accepts the Imam and Mr. Shahabuddin as the exclusive representatives of the Muslim community, religion and culture. For him there are no other shades outside of these, one pure white, the other a deep black, but necessary for the sustenance of the first.

The first point first. The coming of Islam to India from the 10th century on mediated through various agencies—conquerors, theologians, sufi saints, traders, poets, scholars—created several Muslim images of the Hindus, the term itself being of Arabic coinage. For the conquerors, the Hindus were the arch enemy whose territory was open for grabbing through the battlefield. Incidentally, other Muslim rulers too were similar enermies, for their territory had no more sanctity against raids.

Mahmud of Ghazni, the archetypical Muslim conqueror, also had no problem employing 300 Hindu soldiers and one General Tilak for waging wars against other Hindus and they in turn had no problem helping him either. For theologians, the Hindus were kafirs, who needed to be converted to Islam by persuasion or force. For poets, however, kafir was the term of endearment, always used as a synonym for the beloved. Sufis sought love rather than subjugation as the path of salvation for all humankind. Hindus for them were no enemies, but friends. Traders in their turn were more keen on earning their profits from wherever they could and hardly cared about the religious identity of their customers. Of scholars, al-Biruni was the most outstanding, hardly the one who would think of killing or converting the Hindus. But for al-Biruni our knowledge and understanding of the Hindu religion and society of his day would be so much poorer.

All these differential images of the Hindu (and the Muslim) community got erased with the advance of Western analytical categories, and were replaced by homogenised categories such as the Orient as a whole and Christendom, Hindu civilisation, Islamic world, etc. The British, under the influence of both evangelical as well as utilitarian philosophies, made these homogenous categories the premise upon which to establish their governance in India. Mr. Sudarshan is reproducing the ideological constructs of precisely that despicable West he would like India to turn its back upon.

Second, if Mr. Sudarshan could find the determination to look at the Muslim community beyond the shoulders of such stalwarts as the Imam and Mr. Shahabuddin, and acquire some familiarity with the Indian Muslims in the small towns and villages, his complaint that they shun any association with the Hindu cultural legacies would disappear in a jiffy, if that is, he is willing to allow it to disappear. It is here that the vast majority of Indians— Hindus and Muslims and others—live and it is here that the neat boxes into which people such as Mr. Sudarshan tend to fit Hindus and Muslims and Sikhs and Christians and others quickly dissolve.

For, in these villages the Muslims grow up singing Radha and Krishna bhajans and lyrics as integral parts of their lives and celebrate Holi, Dussehra and Diwali as zealously as the Id-ul-Fitr. Indeed, even as they observe the *roza* (fast) during the month of Ramzan and celebrate Id at the end of it, they know much about why Dussehra and Diwali are celebrated.

Mr. Sudarshan might also be astonished to know that it is not entirely a one-side participation in the religous and cultural festivals of the other; in numerous, mainly rural or semi-urban locales, the Hindus also observe several Muslim festivals with equal zeal or solemnity as the occasion demands. This indeed is the basic feature of popular forms of all religions—Hinduism, Christianity, Islam. Where theology tends to be fractious, popular religon is assimilative.

It is not merely that Mr. Sudarshan's familiarity with Indian Islam is very limited; it is the same with Hinduism. Several proselytising religions, Christianity and Islam among them, are premised upon the notion of the final truth being revealed to their prophet. The final truth must in the end vanquish all falsehood. Thus in their respective perceptions, Christianity or Islam must prevail over the entire world some day before the Day of Judgment. Hinduism does not contain the notion of the final truth, hence it is not a proselytising religion and is not predicated upon the notion of final triumph over the others. In his aggressive posing of irresoluble conflict between Hindus, on one hand, and Muslims and Christians, on the other, which implies the ultimate subjugation of the Christians and the Muslims by the RSS-trained and led Hindus, Mr. Sudarshan is abandoning that defining element of Hinduism which has allowed it to survive for several millennia of history.

But then Mr. Sudarshan is aware that systems can be moulded not by the force of truth or logic but by the relations of power and the present dispensation is so perched that his words will carry weight with it, never mind their threat to India's Indian-ness.

Will Digging Resolve the Problem?

The Hindu, 11.3.2003

Let me at the outset state that I for one welcome the directive of the Allahabad High Court for archaeological excavation at the site of the Babri Masjid-Ram Janmabhoomi dispute. The welcome is not in expectation of any definitive resolution of the highly contentious issue, but in the court's implied refusal to accept the validity of the claims of the Sangh Parivar and the Muslim leaders about the existence of a Ram temple underneath the mosque. Even as the denial appears neutral between the two sides, it seems more weighted against the Sangh Parivar if only because it has been the more vociferous of the two in making the claim.

The historical evidence available for a Ram temple having been demolished to build the mosque is extremely slender. The fact that Babur himself records his visit to Ayodhya twice in his *Baburnama* but does not mention either the Ram temple or the construction of a mosque in his name is the first source of doubt about it. The verses carved on the entrance to the prayer hall of the mosque and the inner wall announcing the construction of the mosque, when it was intact, made no mention of the temple either. The fact that silence on the issue reigns among numerous medieval historians of court chronicles, reinforces the doubt significantly.

Some of these historians were dogmatic Muslims, such as Mulla Abdul Qadir Badauni, Akbar's courtier, who would have revelled in recording the incident with great hyperbole. Even Aurangzeb, himself responsible for the demolition of many temples and the construction of mosques on their sites, never mentions the act of his predecessor; this adds significantly to the silence. The several Hindu historians of the period make no reference to it either. But the most deafening silence is that of Goswami Tulsi Das, epitome of devotion to Ram, a resident of Ayodhya, and writing within 50 years of the construction of the mosque, i.e. within living memory of the incident. Nor do the many European travellers, given to a great degree of dramatisation of their narrative, state it with any clarity.

The first clear unambiguous statment that "the Jama Masjid constructed by Emperor Babur at the site of the Birth of Ram, son of Raja Dasrath (is) adjacent to the building of the rasoi (kitchen) of Sita, wife of the above-mentioned Ram" occurs in a Persian language document submitted to the Faizabad law court by its superintendent, Hafizullah, in 1822. Yet, even this document does not mention a temple at the site, demolished for the construction. As the 19th century progressed, gradually an association between the Ramjanmabhoomi and the existence of a Ram temple grew and several disputes began to arise, some of them violent. However, a cardinal principle in the historian's craft is that the value of any piece of textual evidence for testifying the occurrence of an event diminishes with growing distance in time. Evidence of the 19th century will thus be a poor basis to testify an event of the 16th century. Richard M. Eaton, a respected U.S. historian of medieval India, is aware of the Sangh Parivar's ever inflating figures of temples demolished in medieval India and mosques built on their sites, first pegged at 300 some 15 years ago but by now having grown to 30,000. He has meticulously documented the desecration of each and every temple between 1192 and 1760 and arrives at the figure of 80. For details, his paper 'Temple Desecration and Indo-Muslim States' in his book, *Essays on Islam and Indian History*, Oxford University Press, Delhi, 2000, may be consulted. His list does not include the temple at Ayodhya.

If the silences of history leave ambiguous traces on this

count, archaeological evidence by its very nature is slightly less open to varying interpretation, if only relatively. Therefore, the court's directive has the potential of opening the door to a little more substantive evidence on the issue. What are the prospects of this happening?

Some archaeological excavation has already been undertaken around the site by B.B. Lal under the project 'The Archaeology of the Ramayana' in the late 1960s and early 1970s. The fact that he had proposed to extend the excavations further and the non-submission of a final report of his undertaking points to the inconclusive nature of his findings. The court's injunction that further excavations should be carried out in a month's time implies its unfamiliarity with archaeological procedures which are extremely painstaking and time-consuming; a month's digging barely touches the fringe of the site. It is unlikely that such a small amount of digging could yield anything worthwhile.

But even prolonged and extensive digging could yield any of the following scenarios: conclusive evidence that a Ram temple did exist which was demolished to build the temple. It is extremely unlikely that this will happen; but if it does, the Muslim leaders have already announced that they would accept the evidence without further ado and honour it.

Evidence of layers of construction at the site demonstrating buildings of several kinds on top of one another. Very likely at any ancient site. This will seriously puncture the claim that this was the site of Ram's birth and cast doubts on the Sangh Parivar's lifeline campaign. If, on top of it, it also shows that the demolition of an earlier place of worship of a different denomination had preceded the construction of a temple before the mosque—not an unlikely happening in view of the fact that demolition of places of worship of one's political rivals was quite common in history around the world and so too in India and was not specifice to the Muslims—the claim would be damaged even further. No conclusive evidence of the existence of a Ram temple, or any temple, even in the top layers; instead, digging throws up remains of a palace, or a mansion, for example. Not unlikely. This too will seriously strain the Sangh Parivar's claim.

Thus, if the digging bears out the first scenario, the solution will be clear-cut. If not, the matter will no longer be subject to judicial resolution. In the end, it will call for a political solution.

The unearthing of even a slight bit of evidence of a place of worship in the digging might mean a whirlwind campaign unleashed by the likes of Praveen Togadia and Ashok Singhal which will undermine the authority of the Judiciary and seek a forcible solution, helped by the Vajpayee Government's masterly inactivity. We can hardly overlook the fact that the momentum to this agitation was lent by L.K. Advani. The damage to the nation will be incalculable.

The other political solution, ideally to have been attempted in the 1980s, requires a grandeur of vision that the Muslim leadership seems so incapable of: the offer of the site to the Hindus and joining hands with them to build a Ram temple, even if symbbolically. At one stroke, the Sangh Parivar balloon would have burst and the very Indian-ness of Indian Islam would have been established beyond the innuendoes cast on it by Narendra Modi, Mr. Togadia and the like. No one had heard of the Modis and the Togadias then; no one would have heard of them now either. And this one grand gesture would have insured all other medieval mosques against further predatory claims of the Sangh Parivar, some of them with much stronger basis of fact than Ayodhya. Is it too late?

Ayodhya and the Paradox of Indian Polity

The Hindu, 27.6.2003

Like all paradoxes, this paradox too is absolutely breathtaking. The Sangh Parivar, forever on the lookout for proclaiming its 'nationalism' with drumbeats, has made it clear from the word go that it would not honour any judgment of the Indian judiciary on the Ayodhya dispute if it goes against the Hindus. Among the many members of the carefully nurtured multi-tongued Parivar, the VHP, which goes furthest in making claims to being more staunchly nationalist Hindu and Indian than the others within the Parivar or outside is also the most strident in announcing its hostility to the Judiciary. It is followed closely by the RSS, the darling of the Prime Minister and many others at the helm.

The flip side of the claims to being staunch nationalists is the implication that no other group, least of all a community, comes anywhere near it in its commitment to the nation's territorial integrity, its culture and institutions. The Muslims in the Parivar's estimate top the list of those wanting in this commitment; therefore even killing them by the hundreds is an act of patriotism. Yet it is the Muslim community's orthodox leadership that has repeatedly and unreservedly declared its faith in the Indian Judiciary and has announced its commitment to honour the verdict even if it goes against them. This is when none of the judges hearing the case is even a Muslim (not that that by itself would have altered the outcome) and the jurisprudence under which the case is being adjudicated is the secular Constitution of India and not the shariat. Is it easy to imagine anything with a greater irony embedded in it?

The archaeological excavations at the site have thrown up what anyone with the slightest sense of history would have guessed: a mixed lot of evidence, conclusively proving nothing. From the evidence of historical texts and documents it was clear long ago that sustaining the theory of the existence of a Ram temple demolished to build the Babri Masjid in 1528 would be very hard. Twenty-four historians of the JNU had made this very point in 1986 in a very brief, popular pamphlet entitled 'Political Abuse of History'; the pamphlet had raised the issue in public and this had led to some debate in the newspapers. Since then several other bits of writing on the issue have reinforced the historians' doubts. But when have doubts and debates among historians ever been able to prevent politicians from launching forth in *rath yatras* if the *yatras* were expected to lead to ministerial chairs?

In some ways, the Ayodhya dispute is a good pointer to the making of historical 'facts'. While Ayodhya itself is mentioned in medieval Indian texts and while connection between Ayodhya and Ram is also recorded, for example in the *Ain-i-Akbari* of the historian Abul Fazl, written at the end of the 16th century, no one in medieval India has spoken of the existence of a Ram temple demolished to make way for the Babri Masjid. Babur himself records his visit to Ayodhya twice on the same page in his Memoirs, the *Babur nama*, but does not mention a Ram temple nor the mosque built in his name by his general Mir Baqi.

Nor do later historians, some of them very dogmatic Muslims, some others devout Hindus. Nor indeed do poets and writers, either Hindu or Muslim speak of either a Ram temple or the Babri Masjid. Not even Goswami Tulsi Das, Ram's greatest devotee, a resident of Ayodhya and almost an eye witness to the building of the masjid. Nor is there any record of a popular tradition growing in the region linking a particular site with the birth of the Ram, earlier than perhaps the 18th century. For we have a court document of 1822 in the Persian language, submitted to the Faizabad law court by its superintendent, one Hafizullah, testifying that the masjid was built at the site of Ram janmasthan. This is the first evidence establishing the link. Clearly, a tradition had begun to evolve sometime prior to its recording. However, the document still does not speak of a temple, much less of a Ram temple. In the 19th century by and by the story of the existence of a temple there came into circulation and by the 1870s the identification of the temple with Ram had been established. The link between Ram temple and the masjid has a history of no more than 150 years behind it. It has nothing to do with Babur's demolition of an existing Ram temple which the Parivar wishes to restore to salvage the Hindu national pride or at least to fetch votes. And now archaeology has put paid to whatever doubts might have remained on the score of historical records.

However, as the dispute hotted up in the late 1980s, the VHP put up stalls outside the precincts of the masjid and hung garishly coloured tin boards with blood curdling tales, written in grammatically atrocious Hindi, about how every time Babur's masons sought to put a dome on top of the masjid it would collapse. In the end, some mysterious voice spoke to Babur demanding the shedding of the blood of a couple of lakhs of Hindus for the dome to get stabilised. This was duly done and hence the masjid came to be erected. The stories were meant for the benefit of the crowds of visitors, the potential *kar sevaks* as well contributions to the VHP funds; clearly the authors did not need to pitch the stories at any higher level of intelligence, or even grammatically correct language. History was in the making. Perhaps if the Parivar had fetched enough majority by itself in the Lok Sabha this kind of history teaching would have become obligatory in the schools and colleges as well.

In the end of course it is votes that matter not history. Since it is getting clear that Ayodhya wouldn't fetch votes any more—it is very doubtful if it did the last time either—the BJP is willing to become moderate and jettison the strident voices within the Parivar, the VHP in particular. Sibling rivalry at its worst; even so it is good news. For all its bluster, the VHP has no popular support as was evident after the arrest of two of its leading lights in Madhya Pradesh and Rajasthan, when not a blade of grass stirred. The bluster works only under the protection of state power.

Those who understand Indian culture and history—and the VHP is not among them—know that extremism is completely alien to all its religions, be it Hinduism, Buddhism, Jainism, Sikhism or Indian Islam. Occasional bursts of extremist action in these religious communities notwithstanding, no community has a history of sustained support to militant ideology and consequent prolonged violence. It is to this history that India needs to return, not the kind that was inscribed on those garish tin boards at Ayodhya and which VHP leaders like Praveen Togadia and Ashok Singhal still seem to spew at every available opportunity, particularly if there are TV cameras around. The next time you watch a debate on the TV just watch out for the body language of representative participants. The paradox will hit you hard; it would even have been amusing if it were less tragic for the nation.

Parivar's Dilemma

TOI, 24.6.2004

There is no future in the past

That the BJP had raised its strength in Parliament from a miserable two seats in 1984 to 162 in 1999 by focusing its mobilising strategies on Hindutva, is assumed as one of the givens of India's recent past. Its veracity has seldom been scrutinised, or even contextualised. The assumption implies that Hindutva remains an immutable support base for the BJP, and remains ever open to access. It ignores the principle that the same phenomenon yields different meanings when contexts change, leading to differnt consequences.

It follows that the BJP, after its electoral debacle, will revert to its core Hindutva agenda to retrieve the lost ground. The parivar has already charted out this course for the party through strigent VHP voices of protest over the 'deviations' of the last six years. In a slightly more veiled manner, the RSS too has 'advised' the BJP to return to its 'ideological roots' for future survival and growth. If power was the bond that kept different voices muted within the NDA and the parivar, Atal Behari Vajpayee's mastery of ambivalence further helped keep the fissures dormant. Defeat, however, takes the lid off fissures within any family, whether individual or political.

It might therefore be worthwhile to at least contextualise the link between Hindutva and BJP's phenomenal rise to power and equally phenomenal exit from it.

In politics, as in other spheres of life, a party does not enlarge or contract its space due entirely to its own strength or weakness; it does so in competition with others seeking to occupy the same ground. Thus, what 'others' do has a great impact on one's own fortunes. The decline of the Rajiv-led Congress, after the landmark victory of 1984, brought electoral benefits to all non-Congress parties, including the BJP. As non-Congress parties began to work together, tensions arising from the BJP's RSS links began to surface yet again. Matters came to a head when Prime Minister V. P. Singh threw down the gauntlet to the parivar by announcing the Mandal concessions without any prior notice.

L.K. Advani's (in)famous *rath yatra* on the Ayodhya issue—described by Vajpayee even then as 'Advani's yatra' thus distancing himself from it—came in response to that challenge. Since VP had almost conspiratorially mobilised backward and lower castes, caste as the category of political mobilisation, never absent from the Indian scenario, came centre stage. Advani's *yatra,* in turn, encapsulated the response of the BJP's strong upper caste base, which saw itself challenged and outwitted by VP.

In other words, the consolidation of upper crust Hindus under the BJP banner was a reaction. It was no spontaneous popular surge in its favour. In some ways, VP had proved to be the BJP's greatest benefactor.

Once tasting proximity to power through elections, the BJP, however, realised that the Ram temple issue, and Brahmanical ideology, gave it too narrow a base of support and sought to expand it without letting go of either. Hence the need to speak in many voices, and the deliberate elevation of Vajpayee's studiously cultivated ambivalence to the level of statesmanship.

But the direct one-on-one challenge posed by VP has abated and the parivar couldn't find a fantasy demon for its campaign in 2004. It is, therefore, doubtful if a return to strident mobilisation on Ayodhya can bring back the lost glory to the BJP. In politics you can't fight the same battle twice. Yet, this is precisely what the BJP seems intent on doing.

There is a lesson, too, in these developments for the secular intelligentsia. If strident Hindutva has suffered severe setbacks, the Nehruvian atheistic secularism too appears to have suffered the same fate. Through India's long history, the foregrounding of any one religious identity at the level of the state has always had disastrous consequences and led to a redressal of the balance. This was so even in pre-modern times when religion was a predominant presence in society and state.

Thomas Coryat, English traveller to India between 1612 and 1617, has a brilliant anecdote to tell. The only time Mughal emperor Akbar denied anything to his mother, he observes, was when she asked him to order the tying of the Bible around the neck of an ass and have him beaten around the streets of Agra because the Portuguese had tied the *Qur'an* around the neck of a dog in Ormuz and beat him around in the town. What the Portuguese had done, Akbar replied, was awful. But being a king, he could not replicate the same in his kingdom, for "the contempt of any religion is contempt of God".

This is the essence of India that the parivar, like Aurangzeb earlier, sought to alter by propping up one religious identity as the defining element of the state. Atheistic secularism also misses out on the complexity of religious discourse by treating all forms of religious expression as obscurantist a la post-Enlightenment rationality. One does not have to be religious oneself to understand and appreciate the force of religious ideology as a challenge to its communalist transmutation. Medieval India's saint poets understood this, as did Gandhi.

Today, the BJP is at the crossroads, not knowing which way to go. Returning to glory by embracing the past is the surest sign of its lack of self-confidence. Has history ever repeated itself?

Muslim Puzzle

TOI, 29.11.2006

No credible theory to explain mass conversions to Islam

The Muslim question, never out of sight in the Indian context, has again been brought centrestage by the Sachar committee. It is time to look at some of the commonplace assumptions about how the Muslims came to inhabit India in such large numbers—after all, the world's largest Muslim population lives in South Asia. The notion that most of those who converted to Islam in medieval India did so to escape the oppressive Hindu caste system seems to underlie the Sachar committee report.

This theory was lent academic respectablity by a 100-odd page essay in 1952 by Muhammad Habib of the history department of Aligarh Muslim University. Examining the easy victory of the Turkish Muslim invaders of India in early 13th century, Habib inspired by visions of massive popular uprisings in Russia and China in his century, was dismayed by the absence of such resistance in medieval India, and explained it in terms of caste oppression. He felt that the coming of Islam, even at the hands of the decadent Turks, far from inspiring popular defence of India's rulers, was welcomed.

The positive point about this novel explanation was that it brought society into the explanation of a major series of events, distinct from the 'divided rulers' theory. The flaws were many: Its source was a mere two excerpts from

Manusmriti and Al Beruni, separated by several centuries. The assumption that these normative prescriptions reflected society's actual functioning which remained unaltered over centuries, was highly suspect. But there is an even more substantial basis for questioning the theory. If rebellion against the repressive Brahminical caste regime led to the acceptance of Islam as an alternative, one would have expected massive conversions in the heartland of the Hindu orthodoxy: in the northern plains, in Delhi, Uttar Pradesh and Bihar more than anywhere else. Yet, here, according to census reports, the Muslim population never exceeded around 15 per cent. The real mass conversions took place in areas of very weak Brahminical hold: Kashmir valley, Malabar, and what are now Pakistan and Bangladesh.

This brings up the second common assumption: the medieval Muslim state, guided by the binding Islamic precept of converting *kafirs* to Islam, exercising immense power for five and a half centuries, was clearly the chief agency of conversions. This is the favourite hobbyhorse of the Sangh Parivar. History, however, has a strange habit of decimating easy assumptions. If the Gangetic plains comprised the heartland of Brahminical orthodoxy, it was also the core of the highly centralised as well as long lasting Muslim power in medieval times. Yet, massive conversions to Islam occurred in the outlying areas, in the four geographical corners of pre-Partition India, which also comprised the politically peripheral corners of Muslim power in medieval India.

Kashmir valley had turned to Islam long before Akbar had conquered it and Malabar had forever lain beyond the reach of the Muslim state in the north. West Punjab and East Bengal were in a fairly constant state of rebellion which the rulers sitting in Agra or Delhi were seldom able to control for any meaningful length of time. There thus appears to be a clear inverse relationship between Hindu orthodoxy and concentration of political and administrative authority on one hand and regional density of Muslim population on the other. If that were not enough, the available evidence suggests that the heaviest concentration of conversions occurred in a century or so when the British regime had fully established itself in India—between the mid 19th century and 1941 when the last census before Partition was compiled. While one in every six individuals in the subcontinent got converted between the arrival of Islam in India in the 11th century and about 1850, the ratio rose to one in every four in the next century, when Mughal power had long gone.

How about the Sufis, then? While we do get occasional references to conversion being effected by Sufis, even a preliminary review of the itinerary of their migrations would indicate that they were moving from one Muslim-dominated area to another and rarely to a non-Muslim area where conversions could be made. Indeed, when Muhammad bin Tughlaq, before moving his capital from Delhi to Deogiri in Maharashtra suggested that Sufis go and settle in the region to prepare a Muslim base for his arrival, they refused point blank. While practising Islam and spreading its message was central for Sufis, it seems to have fallen way short of any attempt at mass conversions.

We are thus faced with a massive paradox: while the world's largest chunk of Muslim population inhabits the Indian subcontinent, there is not a single work on the process of conversions here. This is largely because we don't have enough data from medieval India for historians to work with. This absence by itself defies any attempt to locate a single, or even a major agency or cause or occasion for mass conversion. We need instead to look for diverse agencies and processes which worked unobtrusively over long stretches of time to turn such huge numbers towards Islam.

Don't Mix Myth and History

TOI, 21.9.2007

Belief in Ram has no bearing on Sethusamundram project

In some ways the controversy about whether Ram actually existed or is a character imagined in a work of fiction takes us back to debates on history in the 19th and a major part of the 20th century. Then the positivist school saw history as an exact science, or at least as having pretensions of being an exact science. It was based on the assumption that the facts of history were as precise and objective as those of the natural sciences and were capable of yielding as unambiguous a meaning. In so doing history was set apart, even set in opposition, to mythology which had no basis as an objective reality.

If the question is posed to a historian or an archaeologist whether Ram actually existed as a historical figure and whether events narrated in the epic Ramayana are to be treated on a par with objective facts, the answer would be a resounding no. The Archaeological Survey of India's famous paragraph submitted in its report to the Supreme Court cannot be faulted on this count.

Historians and archaeologists look for a certain kind of evidence such as historical chronicles, epigraphs, coins and monuments and have a close look at the chronological proximity of the evidence to the events to which they bear witness. The further a piece of evidence from the event is located, the less its value. No evidence of this nature would testify to the historical existence of the figures and events described in epics, just as names, persons, events described in a novel, however realistic, are still imaginary.

However, does it imply that mythology, epics and novels are to be dismissed as unreflective of any kind of reality because the nature of historical evidence does not bear out their existence? Under positivist assumptions, yes. But then positivism itself is far from being the ultimate truth and has suffered severe questioning in recent decades. Mythology, fiction, poetry and paintings relate to a different genre of reality that could for convenience be grouped under culture, of which religion also becomes an important segment, even as the two are far from being synonymous.

In that sense culture and mythology too acquire the characteristics of an objective social reality which governs our attitudes and behaviour. The cultural presence of Ram in India is quite beyond measure in terms of objective history. Even those of us who are devout atheists do not forget to light the lamps on the night of Diwali when the mythological Ram returned from his imaginary exile of 14 years, however we might explain it. The stories from the Ramayana, Mahabharata and various other mythological sources imbibed in our childhood remain part of our cultural subconscious even when we turn away from them in defence of our atheism.

It is also true that there is not one story of Ram and his exile, but several. We only have to see Paula Richman's marvellous book, *The Many Ramayanas,* to appreciate the diversities in the tale. However, the treatment of Ram as a mythological, rather than a historical figure, does not in any way undermine his cultural presence in people's lives. We just have to look around and see the variations of Ram attached to the names of persons, mostly of men, but often also of women, to make a quick assessment of the enormity of his cultural presence. If he were indeed a historical figure, ruling over a minor regional kingdom in Ayodhya, Ram would probably have been relegated to a footnote in a history of the region and forgotten.

Should then this enormous cultural presence of Ram be treated as evidence that the so-called Ram Setu across the sea was actually built by his *vanar sena*? That would hardly be a tenable inference. For, mythology by its very nature is not evidence of historical artefacts, just as the notion of a *pushpak vimana* in the Ramayana is hardly evidence of a flourishing aircraft industry in the time of Ram.

How does the secular Indian state handle issues of this nature? Here it becomes entirely a political question, completely independent of the issues of Ram's historicity or otherwise. One political party, when in power, sanctions the canal project with great fanfare; out of power it smells an opportunity to get rid of its present doldrums, rattle the government and create a popular wave in its favour. All it needs to do is to stage a few demonstrations and TV channels and newspapers lap them up.

The Indian electorate has shown on several occasions that it is not willing to be swayed by issues of this nature. Remember the defeat of the BJP in the Hindi belt in the wake of the demolition of the Babri Masjid? If the UPA government has the will to call the Sangh Parivar's bluff on Ram Setu, it could still go ahead with the project after satisfying the Supreme Court. But the government went down on its knees even as the first few pictures of a few score protestors appeared on the TV screens. It was Indian democracy at its worst.

Minority Report

TOI, 26.11.2007

The unwillingness to face the challenge of minority communalism is now coming home to roost. An obscure body claiming to speak for Muslims has called Kolkata's secular credentials into question. It was more keen to ensure the expulsion of Taslima Nasreen from the city than resettle the displaced refugees of Nandigram.

The West Bengal government and Left parties will explain it away as the work of anti-social elements, if not that of some Islamic militants from across the border. But the fact that a number of people responded to the call and played havoc with life in the city stands out over and above these explanations. We are paying the price for underrating the threat of minority communalism. Now, it has assumed proportions serious enough to pose a threat to government that projected itself as the chief protector of minorities.

'Secular' mobilisation has lent strength to the notion that while all communalism is bad, majority communalism poses a much greater threat to the nation than minority communalism. We are left with only majority communalism as a strong adversary. The 'secular' parties' unwillingness to question, challenge and confront minority communalism has thus created a space for it to grow, as its leaders realise the power vested in it as a political force or vote bank. Almost all parties have contributed to this growth: the Sangh Parivar by posing a threat to the physical existence of Muslims, the Congress by playing up this threat, the Left by underplaying minority communalism and the liberal Muslim intelligentsia by harping on Muslim Personal Law and so forth.

There have been voices of dissent within the Muslim community. Rajiv Gandhi's minister Arif Mohammad Khan was against surrendering to the demands of dogmatic mullahs on the Shah Bano case in the 1980s. He even resigned from the government when Rajiv Gandhi decided to go ahead and defy the Supreme Court in the hope of cornering Muslim votes. Khan lost the election.

But these are lone, individual voices, pitted against not only the orthodox leadership within the Muslim community but almost every government. In the absence of a larger social movement, the orthodox leadership's hold on the Muslim community has increased. The expansion of political space for the assertion of communal identity has only helped conservative elements. Secular parties including the Left, abet such tendencies by their silence.

Given these developments, some of the assumptions of India's modernisation project can be called into question. Jawaharlal Nehru's enthusiasm for parliamentary democracy was based on his perception that colonial exploitation had left India and its people 'backward' vis-à-vis the indices of modernity—industrial economy, education and political awareness. Hence, they fell back upon their pre-modern identities of caste, community and religion.

It was believed that industrialisation, bringing together workers of all religions and castes, will obliterate their pre-modern mindset and forge a new collective identity of class. Modern education was expected to raise them above pre-modern identities. The experience of parliamentary democracy, where each individual is left alone before the ballot box, with the symbolic withdrawal of all extraneous controls—those of the family, the community, and caste—was expected to act as a catalyst for creating modern political sensibilities.

All this has not happened. Casteism, communalism and regionalism have never been stronger as a political force. The clash between secularism and communalism has come to imply multi-community mobilisation as opposed to single community mobilisation.

If the majority and minority communalisms are left to challenge each other, it is hard to imagine a greater disaster awaiting India, for their mutual challenge leads to mutual reinforcement. As a fallout of the happening in Kolkata, one can visualise one man laughing all the way to his vote bank: Narendra Modi in far off Gujarat.

Two Sides of the Same Coin

TOI, 10.10.2008

Majority, minority communalism feed off each other

On the communalism front, two divergent yet complementary strategies seem to be under way in India, both inspired by utter contempt for the nation's democratic polity as well as for the country's historical and cultural traditions: one envisioned and undertaken by the Sangh Parivar, the other by the various arms of minority communalism.

On the one hand, the Sangh Parivar, working through its myriad branches, has learnt its lesson well from the Nazi experiment: gradually spread communalism in society's nooks and corners, come to power in the states, and, under the government's protection go all out to wreak on the social fabric an unambiguous, aggressive communal divide. Using their various organisations like the RSS and the Bajrang Dal, they unleash vicious and often wild propaganda against the minorities and organise riots, kill people and demolish properties. The perpetrators move with the confidence that when the state acts it will be on their behalf.

The law of the land is the last concern on their minds. Indeed, Narendra Modi has demonstrated through the travesty of truth that goes under the name of the Nanavati Commission that law should be treated like an ass. Once you have succeeded in creating durable fissures in society through long, sustained hard work, political power follows in its wake even in a free and fair election. Elections won, the rule of law can be laughed at in different forums. The Parivar has had to effect an improvement on the Nazi experiment here: it can claim electoral legitimacy for all its illegitimate actions. But the essence is the same—power remains the central feature. Law will always be its servant. If some day the Parivar were to capture full control of the state in New Delhi, all its virulent constituents could be given free run.

Minority communalism, on the other hand, does not go by any of these pretences. Terror is its chosen weapon. The more the Parivar succeeds in marginalising and 'punishing' the minorities by using the state's organs, the more legitimacy it creates in the minds of militancy's adherents and followers. Even its failure to create widespread communal tensions by carrying out terror strikes on temples, mosques, bazaars and streets does not seem to deter it. Its strategy is to persevere in this endeavour and wait for simmering tensions to grow until they reach a tipping point. Conversely, militancy of the minority in turn lends force to the Parivar. It is thus that the Parivar and militant minority communalism are each other's firmest allies.

But then minority communalism is not the by-product of the Sangh Parivar's politics alone, even though militancy may have been fed by the Parivar's strigency. Indeed, it has a much longer history, although it does not go back to India's five and a half medieval centuries, when the Muslims ruled over much of the land. In fact, this period was remarkably free of communal rioting, as we understand the phenomenon today.

The first recorded riot occurred in 1683 in Ahmedabad, when Muslim rule was nearing its end, and the whole of the 18th century was witness to five cases of rioting. In the later 19th century and especially in the 20th, on the one hand a 'siege mentally' grew among Muslims and on the other the freedom struggle, which mobilised masses of people, reinforced the siege mentality. This resulted in the country's partition.

Since Independence, such an attitude has found strength

in various sources and challenges from none. If there was the constant RSS–Jan Sangh and subsequent BJP threat, the Congress has revelled in keeping this threat alive to corner the Muslim vote. The community's own leadership too had a strong stake in indulging in rhetoric, and its liberal leaders never tired of crying themselves hoarse at the supposed 'decline' of Urdu, etc.

The Left, ideologically most well-equipped to contest communalism, made a very questionable distinction between majority and minority communalism on the plea that the former alone was capable of turning fascist. Hence one could overlook the latter. In the process, it ignored the integral link between the two, with one feeding off the other. The result: the Left could effectively challenge neither.

Today, as a feeling of helplessness of the state and the citizens seems to stare us in the face, the writing appears on the wall highlighting two requisites. Since it is the state's exclusive responsibility to deal with acts of disturbance of law and order and of terror, any strong, but impartial action by it to combat these can only earn it support from all citizens, belonging to all communities. The assumption that such strong action will antagonise one community or another is, among other things, grossly unfair to that community, for terrorism threatens us all equally.

Secondly, voice of opposition to terror and of acts of communal frenzy, still somewhat feeble within each community must grow much louder in the form of actual mass mobilisation, not only against the other's communalism but also that of one's own community. That includes the minority communities.

One of a Kind

TOI, 20.12.2008

Indian Muslims are a unique community

The distinctiveness of Indian Muslims is asserting itself again. Over the past few months Muslim theologians distanced themselves from what has come to be branded 'Islamist terror' in the media followed by an organised expression of unqualified disapproval by as many as 6,000 ulema from around the country gathered in Hyderabad specifically for the purpose. This highlights the distinctiveness of Indian Muslims which has evolved through centuries of Indian history. There is probably no other instance of the ulema rising up in protest against terrorism on this scale anywhere else in the world. And in the wake of the Mumbai attacks, ordinary as well as elite Muslims also gave public went to their outrage.

To apopreciate this distinctiveness, it is instructive to look at the process of conversions to Islam that took place in India. The Muslims inhabiting the Indian subcontinent comprise the largest concentration of the community in the world. The easiest assumption, is that conversions were effected by the might of the medieval Muslim state in India over the six centuries that it ruled. Yet, interestingly there is not a single book on the subject of conversion in India as a whole. There are two books on the subject in Kashmir, another on Bengal. That's it. The reason is that there is not enough historical evidence to substantiate a book length work. This in turn implies that conversion did not take place at the hands of one agency or at one go or for one reason, either by the use of force or temptation or persuasion. For, if such had been the case, there was no way it could have escaped being recorded either by Islamic scholars or their opponents.

Indeed, the geographical distribution of the density of Muslim population in the subcontinent flies in the face of the notion that the medieval Indian state could have been even the chief agency of conversion. The highest density is located in four geographical peripheries of the subcontinent: the Kashmir valley in the north, Pakistan in the west, Bangladesh in the east and in the Malabar region down south. That is where the Muslims are, and were, in a majority. These were also the political peripheries of the medieval Muslim state. Kashmir had turned to Islam long before the medieval Indian state reached there in Akbar's reign. West Punjab was a land where the hold of the medieval state was forever disputed and tenuous. East Bengal was seldom under the control of Delhi or Agra either and the Muslim state's reach never extended to Kerala anyway.

On the other hand, in the heartland of the Muslim empire—Bihar, U.P., Delhi, East Punjab—for nearly six centuries the Muslims never exceeded around 15 per cent of the total population. Significantly, the massive conversions amounting to about a 50 per cent rise—from about one in six to one in four of the population—occurred between the second half of the 19th century and 1941, the last census before the Partition, when the British ruled here. And overall, a fraction less than 25 per cent of the population had converted from the arrival of Islam in India to about the time of the Partition.

Massive as these conversions are, two things stand out: if the medieval Indian Muslim state had taken upon itself the role of the religious zealot, it could not have been satisfied with converting just about one in every six inhabitants; and, the process of conversion was so slow, spread out over such long stretches of time and almost imperceptible that medieval historians and litterateurs, both Hindu and Muslim, failed to notice and record it, except as sporadic events.

It is this slow, stretched out process that explains the persistence of a wide spectrum of pre-Islamic, sometimes even anti-Islamic, customs, ceremonies, values and mores among the converts. Historian Ghulam Ahmad Tabtabai, writing in the 1780s, noted that the Muslims celebrated Holi as much as the Hindus. And Mirza Qateel a little later said that except for the Afghans and fanatics among Muslims, everyone played Holi and celebrated Diwali. But much more significant is the fact that militancy has never found much civil support either among the Hindus or Indian Muslims. It, therefore, becomes understandable that all the assaults on temples, mosques and dargahs in the past few years with the clear intention of inflaming communal passions and inciting violence have failed to provoke a single incident of rioting.

The Indian Muslims are thus a part of that all-encompassing civilisation of which tolerance of difference is a central feature. The offence that Islamic militants have caused to this civilisation and to the Muslims in the process is now being confronted with protests from within the community.

One happy result of these happening is the gradual lifting of the siege mentality with which Indian Muslims have lived for a long time. The seeping realisation that peace lies in reaching out, rather than sulking in isolation from the other communities, bodes well for us all. It has the capability to erode the hold of other forms of communalism as well.

Faith No Bar

TOI, 8.5.2009

Inclusiveness is the guiding tenet of Indian Secularism

Used as we were in India to the horrifying spectacle of frequent communal riots every year, it is some relief to note that the recent past for over a decade and a half has been relatively free of this recurring nightmare. The last big spurt of rioting occurred in early 1993 in (then) Bombay in the wake of the demolition of the Babri masjid in far off Ayodhya. Since then, barring the massacre of Muslims in Gujarat in February 2002, there has been relative quiet on this front, despite grave provocation by way of bomb blasts in temples, mosques, dargahs and markets. What could possibly explain this descent of sanity?

On December 6, 1992, when the Babri masjid was demolished by those bearing allegiance to the sangh parivar, for many of us reared in the tradition of secularism posited on the separation of religion and state which bordered on atheism, the world crashed. All the values that we had held dear were under attack. Then, by and by news began to filter through in the papers that in one small town here, another big village there, common people, local Hindus and Muslims, had together undertaken to rebuild the temples and mosques damaged or destroyed in the wake of the events at Ayodhya.

Stories also reported that during the riots, several devout Hindus and Muslims had given shelter and succour to people of the other community. What marked out the denouement this time round was the combination of individual acts of humanity and generosity and collective and joint intervention to rebuild the religious structures, and to undertake to prevent their recurrence in their locality. Hope began to revive.

But the renewal of hope also raised questions about the nature of secularism in the Indian context. To understand it, we might distinguish between a proselytising religious (or non-religious) ideology and a non-proselytising one. Christianity, Islam and Marxism belong to the first category and Hinduism, to the second. A proselytising ideology is predicated upon its monopoly of the final truth, which by definition marks out all else as falsehood. Also implicated is inevitable conflict, and one ideology's ultimate universal triumph over all falsehoods. Triumph is embedded in the notion of the Day of Judgment, common to Christianity and Islam. Marxism also predicted the inevitable universal victory of socialism, and then communism one day.

Association with, and the use of, state power for that triumph is almost a condition. The spread of Christianity, Islam and Marxism were all aided by the state. However, post-Enlightenment, Christian society began to postulate separation between the church and the state, but not between religion and state. Muslim societies never accepted this separation and still do not. It is only the collapse of the erstwhile socialist regimes in the Soviet Union and elsewhere that has snapped the ties between Marxism and the state.

Hinduism does not formulate the notion of the final truth and, therefore, its ultimate universal triumph either through persuasion or conflict. On the contrary, it creates space for a great diversity of opinions and beliefs and their coexistence. It is the overwhelming presence of this ethos in India that also moderates others' zeal which marks out the all-encompassing Indian civilisation. The concept of either identification of religion and state or their separation did not have much relevance here.

At the popular level, this found utterance in the very moving poetry of medieval India's saint poets, both Hindu and Muslim. Theirs was essentially religious poetry, but one that encompassed universal religiosity in lieu of sectarian religions. In some ways, this tradition was pitted against any form of atheism, even as there was a strong atheistic streak in Hindu philosophy, so eloquently highlighted by the late Professor Debiprasad Chattopadhyay in several of his writings. It was this ideology of universal religiosity that preserved social peace in India's medieval centuries, when the first recorded communal riot occurred only towards the end of the Muslim rule, in Ahmedabad, in 1683.

These are the values Mahatma Gandhi encapsulated in his personal as well as political conduct, which people in small towns and villages invoked when they undertook to rebuild damaged places of worship. This value system brought back peace in a highly fractured society. Atheistic secularism had lost ground substantially.

This is the ethos that is an eyesore for the sangh parivar, which models itself on the proselytising religions, and is keen to mobilise state power for achieving the ultimate victory of its version of Hindutva, the very antithesis of Hinduism, if indeed there is such a thing. For, we should remember that even the term Hindu is of Arabic origin.

Can this inclusive tradition survive the multifarious assaults on it? Optimism may derive strength from the fact that it has survived many severe assaults on it in the past, not least the partition of the country on religious grounds. However, caution is still in order inasmuch as history also records drastic changes everywhere. And these are inclusive of changes in people's mindsets, relationships and, not least, faiths.

P.S. Personally I still remain a devout atheist.

III. Book Reviews

Frank's New World

The Express Magazine, 15.11.1998

Andre Gunder Frank, *ReOrient: Global Economy in the Asian Age,* Vistaar, New Delhi.

If challenging received wisdom is a trademark of Andre Gunder Frank's intellectual endeavour, what with his earlier work on the structuring of underdevelopment of the colonised world in the very process of development of the West, this book is written as the mother of all challenges. At the end of it, one is left a little numb at the forced realisation that all history taught around the world over the 19th and 20th centuries was not 'Real History', but rather 'Eurocentric Social Theory', the theme of the first chapter which is repeated relentlessly through the book. It was all constructed under European streetlights, a phrase repeated nearly a dozen times.

The challenge begins with the title itself: Historians must learn henceforth to Reorient themselves, indeed strictly to Reorient towards the Orient. For, in history, especially between 1400 and 1800, the world economy was indeed a global economy with Asia's slice in production and trade being the lion's share.

Much of the modern historiography around the world has for its perspective the rise of capitalism in the West over the past four centuries; the history of the world, especially 'medieval' history comes into focus only in this perspective. All of 'medieval' history thus becomes 'modern' history's, that is, modern European history's 'other'. Frank does not make the point specifically, but would probably have no quarrel with it, and he seeks to stand this perspective on its head.

The Eurocentric perspective was constructed by the great masters of social 'science' (Frank's citation marks), Karl Marx and Max Weber in particular, and some of the most influential historians/sociologists of our age — Fernand Braudel, Immanuel Wallerstein and, not least, Frank himself. Indeed, in his account, other masters before them, like Herodotus and Adam Smith, had been far more sensitive to the global nature of world history. "It was only the nineteenth-century Europeans who literally rewrote the history from their Eurocentric perspective," says Frank.

Whether in Marx's study of all history leading to the development of capitalism, or Weber's spotlighting Protestant ethics for the rise of the West and its dominance of the world, Braudel's teleological location of Europe's onward march from the Middle Ages, Wallerstein's construction of the Modern World System, or Frank's own former vision of the development of underdevelopment, everywhere, modern Europe's presence is the vantage point from which the past is perceived.

In this book, Frank constructs a vision of a "single world economy with a worldwide division of labour and multilateral trade from 1500 onward". Asia dominated that economy until about 1750, or even 1800. "Europe remained a marginal player in the world economy with a perpetual deficit despite its relatively easy and cheap access to American money, without which Europe would have been almost entirely excluded from any participation in the world economy," Frank avers.

Step by step, Frank elaborates and fleshes out this argument. During the period 1400 to 1800, "The two major regions that were most central to the world economy were India and China. That centrality rested primarily on their outstanding absolute and relative productivity in manufactures." Between the two regions, China was more central than India, though India came a close second.

If Europe had no manufactures to sell to Asia, it had gained access to the bullion, particularly silver resources of the Americas. With these, Europe bound up the world trade network with a new thread, exchanging it with gold in China, and with manufactures in China and India. Frank demolishes "the hoarding thesis", propounded in the West by scholars, among others, from David Hume to Adam Smith, to Wallerstein, down to Charles Kindelberger: "The money was dug up in the West only to be buried again in the East." The implicit dichotomy in the thesis between the "economic rationality" of the West and the "irrationality" of the East appals Frank and, in two well-researched chapters, he establishes that the new American money raised prices in Europe and production and population in Asia. "In 1750, Asia's still less than 66 percent of world population produced 80 per cent of the world's GNP. That suggests that Asians must have been *more* productive than Europeans." (Enphasis Frank's)

How did Europe come to rule the world economically (and politically) in the 19th century and the first half of the 20th? What, in other words, explains the "rise of the West", a phrase Frank abhorns? The break came somewhere between 1750 and 1800, or even 1850. "The most important answer is that Europeans obtained the money from the gold and silver mines they found in the Americas." They invested it in slave plantations in those very regions and sold their products to the Americans themselves. This gave economic and technological muscle to Europe, further reinforced by the import of slave labour from Africa. The rising profits allowed Europeans to *buy into* the wealth of Asia itself. (Emphasis Frank's)

American money, rather than any "superior, ethnic, rational, organisational or spirit-of-capitalist advantages" gave Europe the upper hand. Indeed, it was "the advantage of 'backwardness' afforded by their position at the (semi) periphery of the world economy" that accounts for the

European triumph in the two recent centuries. It forced Britain, leader of the Industrial Revolution, to invent technology that could find its products a place in the competitive world market.

In terms of Kondriatieff's long cycles of expansion and contraction, the A and the B phases, from the 1760s, the B phase squeezed European economics of profits both at home and abroad; this also generated the inventions of the Industrial Revolution in the last third of the 20th century, which gave Europe the edge. "The simultaneous progressive weakening of Asian economies—for whatever reasons—offered opportunities and incentives to some regions and sectors in Europe to intervene. They reduced their costs of production through labour and energy generating inventions." Asia, on the other hand, was caught in Mark Elvin's "high equilibrium trap": the high productivity of labour, and its cheapness and abundance, inhibited technological innovation.

But then, like all historical phenomena, the West's ascendancy is transitory: "Why Did The West Win (Temporarily)?" is the title of the penultimate chapter. Already, there are sure signs of the cycle turning the full circle, with the economic revival of the four Asian tigers—South Korea, Taiwan, Hong Kong and Singapore—and, above all, China. Indeed, all this leads Frank to philosophise on whether historians should not return to the earlier cyclical rhythm of time, and abandon linear time, itself a product of European thought of the two centuries. At any rate, methodologically, history perceived in terms of "holism, commonality and continuity" is a much better alternative to one captured in parts, with breaks and dominance.

At the end of the book, one experiences breathlessness, what with the sweep of the argument and its all-questioning and all-encompassing nature and not least its passion. Its grandeur is not diminished by its polemics, nor by the several very weak flanks. The "high equlibrium trap", on which a good half of his argument rests, is one such. Abundance of cheap labour does not by itself inhibit labour-saving inventions, as Joseph Needham had shown years ago in *The Great Titration*. Indeed, this segment of Frank's argument is part of a surprisingly unchallenged received wisdom. Its obverse side, the advantages of backwardness for Europe, would turn suspect on similar grounds.

The inspiration that drove him to write the book, the rise of the four Asian tigers, also would render some of his glowing optimism about the cyclical rhythm of history a shade dimmer, in view of the current problems in some of the regions. But then, the immense power of the book rests on its ability to provoke and force one to rethink many facets of history that had been taken for granted for a long, long time.

Legacy of Marxism

Social Sceintist, Vol. 18, Nos. 8-9, August-September 1990

Randhir Singh, *Of Marxism and Indian Politics,* Ajanta Publications, Delhi, 1990, pp. 80.

This slim volume comprises stray pieces put together by Professor Randhir Singh, one of the major radical intellectuals of our times. The opening piece, 'In lieu of a bio-data' is a delightful all-too-brief autobiographical note, talking less of the author than of the formation of a political commitment that was to last a lifetime and in which the light still glows. A lonely son of prosperous parents, he learnt his lessons in defiance of authority, not petty authority, but the state itself, that took him through life's whole spectrum of vicissitudes, his idealism never flagging. It also seems to have given him a rare sense of humour, which perhaps made the vicissitudes more bearable.

The other bits are Professor Singh's interventions mostly in response to questions raised in the course of carrying out his political commitments or at seminars. His strong adherence to the basic tenets of Marxism runs through all his interventions. The basic tenet in his conception is that it is the economic structure of a society that sets the limits to the freedom of human choice and that therefore the question of class remains central to any analysis of Indian, or for that matter, any other society today. He sets out this perspective in two early theoretical articles, 'Of Marxism Today' and 'Politics—The Dialectics of Science and Revolution in Karl Marx'. However, these are no mere assertions, no *obiter dicta:*

the case is argued right to the end against eclecticism of all sorts even when it is placed forward as Marxist. But Professor Singh is never crass, never oblivious of the multiple mediations which articulate themselves in the course of the articulation of class struggle as the basic mode of social functioning and social change. The class structure sets out the framework of human choices; there is, however, nothing inevitable about a particular choice throwing itself up and displacing others; there is nothing inevitable in human history, not even socialism. The ultimate makers of history are therefore human beings themselves, not any given 'force' or 'forces'.

It is in this perspective that the next three essays, 'Marxists and the Sikh Extremist Movement in Punjab', 'Theorising Communalism in India' and 'Visions for the Future: One View' have been written. Professor Singh forcefully questions what he repeatedly terms the traditional nationalist version of communalism which treats communalism 'above all as an ideology', doesn't matter even if it throws in economy, class, false consciousness and what have you for good measure. For, fundamentally what it loses sight of is the class structure of Indian society and therefore the perspective that communalism is a strategy of the ruling classes; the solution to the problem does not therefore lie in sermonising on secularism to the people but in seeking to transform that class structure. The same perspective permeates his 'Vision for the Future', an intervention in a seminar organised by the ICSSR on the theme.

Professor Singh presents his arguments with force, passion and humour; these are also arguments combining, in the words of one of his students, both idealism and intelligence. His information is always remarkably up-to-date and he always turns his information into knowledge, and an instrument of social change. He also has the humility to realise the limits of intellectuals' effort to change society for a better future, for society will indeed be changed by those who need the change most. But "we make our effort where we work, or we make no effort at all", as he so movingly puts it.

Salutary as Professor Singh's presentation is, some questions do trouble one as one goes along. With all the qualifications that he has added to the *ultimately* determining role of the economic base, it still involves the question of a kind of inverse teleology: the economic base would give the rationale of a phenomenon like communalism, for example, and transformation of that base should at least create the conditions for the solution of that problem. We have the experiment of such a transformation in the socialist world and yet problems akin to communalism have remained intact there. The argument that the assumption underlying those experiments, that the change in the base by itself would change the consciousness of human beings, was a questionable one is valid by itself. It perhaps follows then that in social analysis there is no *permanent* hierarchy of causes, no ultimate rationale. This is not to argue in favour of factor analysis, but to suggest that each conjuncture may perhaps have its own hierarchy and therefore each may require its own solution of problems. Anyway, Singh's arguments wouldn't be worth the while if they did not provoke questioning! It is in this mode that he inherits the true legacy of Marxism.

There is a certain poetic quality about the pieces: the total absence of either bitterness or regret at seeing so much of failure of so much of what one had held dear, the refusal to bow to the innumerable opportunities of cooption offered by the system and above all the lyrical core of an undying optimism. It is therefore not surprising that Professor Singh's first book was a book of Punjabi poetry.

Two Academics Trace India's Green History

Down to Earth, 31.8.1992

Madhav Gadgil and Ramachandra Guha, *This Fissured Land,* Oxfod University Press, New Delhi, 1992.

This book by two of India's most eminent environmental historians makes a first attempt at constructing an alternative, ecological view of Indian history. Coming on the heels of Clive Ponting's *A Green History of the World,* this is a very welcome first step.

The book is divided into three sections: The theoretical perspective, an outline of the history (and, briefly, sociology) of pre-modern India from an ecological view and a fairly detailed account of conflicts over forest from the days of colonial rule till the present time.

Part I establishes the salience of an ecological vision and its methodology, projected backwards. In essence, it posits Modes of Resource Use (MRU) as an alternative to Modes of Production (MOP) methodology, although the authors insist on complementarity, rather than conflict, between the two. The history of MRU is marked out in four stages: hunting-gathering, pastoralism, settled agriculture and industry.

The emphasis on complementarity between MRU and MOP more than repays an old debt to Marxism. In fact, Marxism of a somewhat questionable kind permeates a good deal of the analysis—perhaps accidentally in the history of MRU and MOP, but intentionally in locating a "dominant mode within a socio-ecological formation" which would not "preclude the existence of more than one mode..."(p. 13), in a somewhat deterministic attribution of changes in rituals, ideology and social organisation to changing MRU (pp. 29, 34). This does hamper the emergence of a full-fledged, alternative, compelling vision rooted in the ecological perspective. Even so, the departure the authors make, however half-heartedly, is still useful.

Part II is perhaps the weakest in the book—and not for reasons of brevity alone. First, there is far too much speculation for the historian's empiricist liking: "... there may have been a fall in agricultural production..." and so on, although the lack of evidence is admitted.

Second, the story of the ancient past is a virtual carbon copy of the somewhat dated historiography of R.S. Sharma, which visualises declining trade and currency in circulation deurbanisation and receding agriculture between the fourth and tenth centuries, which comprises the "early medieval period". Each of these postulates has been knocked down by a host of recent works and the notion of a "a major resource crunch" in these centuries (p. 92) has been revised by Sharma himself who now speaks of "a great agrarian expansion and higher yield" in the period in a piece of writing that has not been referred to. And the whole of medieval India for which according to the authors, "excellent records exist" (p. 107) has been dismissed in just two perfunctory paragraphs.

Finally, this section is short on sensitivity—unlike Part III—in dealing with the power relationship between the state and society. Thus, it is assumed with too easy facility that the Mauryan state was able to enforce the exclusion of elephant meant for the diet of forest tribes (p. 86), while the British and post-Independence states have faced continual resistance from the tribes while enforcing their laws.

Not surprisingly, it is in Part III, which deals with the colonial and post-colonial periods, that the book comes alive, although it focusses only on the forest. The perspective is clear, the treatment detailed, sensitive and multi-faceted and the overall statement is made with passion.

There is a basic question all ecologist have to face; Must concern for environmental protection imply compromising current or future material well being? If this is the only workable dichotomy we can posit, where do we go from here?

In answer to the question, they have merely summarised the current debate on the subject in half a page. The question therefore still remains: Where do we go from here?

Stuck in a Groove

Biblio, July 1995

Irfan Habib, ***Essays in Indian History: Towards a Marxist Perception,*** **Tulika, New Delhi, 1995 pp. 389.**

One amongst several cultural creations of medieval India was the tradition of writing a certain kind of history, today characterised as court-history. The positioning of the historian, invariably a courtier, gave him a two-fold perspective of history which runs through all the works that have been handed down to us, their enormous mutual differences notwithstanding: the focus of their intellectual reconstruction was the events at the court, what with all the stories of the accession of rulers, their victories and defeats, the intrigues of the nobles, deposition or death of rulers etc.; and being witness and often participants in the events of the contemporary court that formed their narrative, the perspective of historical causation lay for them in individual, human volition, which was transferred on to the events of the distant past as well. The events that constituted the narrative of a particular reign were a mere reflection of the will or disposition or at best the nature of the ruler. This perspective was in sharp contrast to the assumptions that underlay medieval European historiography where the historian was also the priest and visualised historical causation in terms of divine will alone. Ever since the medieval centuries in India, the court histories continued to constitute not merely the source of data but also the prototype of virtually all historical works. Most of the works that were, and are still read in the teaching and research syllabi of medieval history are patterned after the court histories in their focii as well as in their historical explanation. Hence, a series of books dealing with a succession of medieval dynasties, explaining history in terms of the ruler's will or disposition or nature. Indeed, the prototype well extended across the temporal zones of Indian history.

A major historiographical transition, however, occurred between the mid-1950s and mid-1960s, though an earlier initiative had been taken by A.R. Desai in *The Social Background of the Indian National Movement,* first published in 1948. The paradigm shift came with D.D. Kosambi's *An Introduction to the Study of Indian History,* 1956, followed by Irfan Habib's *Agrarian System of Mughal India,* 1963 and R.S. Sharma's *Indian Feudalism,* 1965. The paradigm shift had a decisive and assertive inclination towards the Marxist analytical frame in terms of modes of production in which the will, nature, disposition of individual rulers or for that matter the outcomes of individual battles here and there were brushed aside in the all-engulfing sweep of societies, peoples, masses in transition.

The intervention of Irfan Habib in 1963 was thus on one hand part of this decisive moment; but in several ways it constituted that decisive moment itself. If, in concert with the endeavour of other influential historians, Habib set new terms of debate in Indian historical writing, he also set new standards of research with his wide ranging, yet meticulous search for detail and equally meticulous recording of history on a grandiose scale, with a totalising explanation. It constituted the most forceful assertion of what came to be regarded as the arrival of 'scientific' and 'secular' history writing in India. It was scientific because it was objective; it was objective because it was based on verifiable, acknowledged data; it was secular because it explained history in terms of class struggle rather than in terms of either religious, sectarian or even individual contestations, which had all pre-modern, backward looking, subjective moorings.

From 1963 to around mid-1980s, Habib went on to explore several other areas of research as the essays collected in this volume, but all of them published elsewhere, demonstrate. One rubric which also bore the mark of Habib's breathtaking scholarship, i.e., the history of technology is for some unexplained reason missing from this anthology.

The first two essays in this volume, 'Problems of Marxist Historiography' and 'Marx's Perception of India' are obviously theoretical in nature. The first makes a very valuable exploration of the problem of contradictions of socialism in a somewhat heretical vein, emphasising the necessity of recognising that contradictions did not end with the end of capitalism in the then USSR and that these contradictions called for analysis in Marxist terms, which he asserts can best be performed by historians of the socialist countries. That was in 1988. The second essay both questions and reaffirms in turn several of Marx's observations on India and is reverential towards some of Marx's prescriptions for its future.

'The Social Distribution of Landed Property in Pre-British India: A Historical Survey', first published in 1965, was an important, empirically sound thesis about the high degree of economic stratification prevalent in pre-British rural society. Habib had in 1963 already challenged the hegemonic Marxist assumption of the absence of private property in land in early and medieval India; this essay provided the flesh to that challenge.

'The Peasant in Indian History' 1982, repeats much of the data and all of the argument that Habib had already put forward in his book and several other essays on the theme, as indeed does 'Forms of Class Struggle in Mughal India', 1980. One of the most stimulating explorations of Habib came in 'Potentialities of Capitalistic Development in the Economy of Mughal India', 1968. In this piece, Habib took on a major orthodoxy of the Marxist historians of India, particularly the Russian historians, namely, the great potential of the development of capitalism in the late Mughal economy of

India, in view of the large space occupied by commercial capital. If the development of industrial capitalism was thwarted here, the blame squarely rested with the intervention of British colonialism. Habib, following Marx's classic insights, argued that commercial capital could subsist with any mode of production and could not therefore by itself be the agency of change. It was the internal articulation of a mode of production, i.e., the contradictions inherent in the production system rather than trade which brought about historical transition. With this insight as the perspective, Habib did a detailed and magnificent analysis of medieval India's mode of production and argued that irrespective of colonial intervention, capitalism didn't have a chance in India!

The significance of the piece on 'Caste in Indian History' is in as much as Marxist historians have usually overlooked the problematic of caste in their anxiety to establish the hegemony of class as the analytical tool, which supercedes the other existential categories of caste, community etc. Habib, does consider the problematic of caste, but in the end reduces it to a form of class "Being a relatively rigid form of division of labour, the caste system formed part of the relations of production." It does not help much to explain the resilience of the caste system which has survived slavery, R.S. Sharma's 'feudalism', colonialism and modern capitalism, even Jyoti Basu's and Irfan Habib's socialism!

Three other essays deal with the question of colonialism: 'Processes of Accumulation in Pre-colonial and Colonial India', 'Colonialisation of Indian Economy 1757-1900' and 'Studying a Colonial Economy—Without Perceiving Colonialism', which is a scathing damnation of *The Cambridge Economic History of India*, Vol. II, edited by Prof. Dharma Kumar. All of them are rich, if partial, in data and reinforce the exploitative part of Marx's paradigm on colonialism.

The essays published here and elsewhere demonstrate Habib's extremely impressive range of research interests, command over data and mastery of elegant style. However, all of them, particularly the ones that pertain to medieval history, merely reaffirm the finality of his basic research of 1963. If the paradigm of the 1950s and 1960s has recently undergone a severe strain and questioning, Habib might well say, "Damn the questioning, for the younger scholars know not what they do"! If newer paradigms have evolved, Habib would not even consider them, even if only to challenge, but would rather let them "pass me by". It is queer for a Marxist, forever fighting for changing society (inevitably the first quotation from Marx in this volume, is the opening sentence, "the point is to change it") being so firmly committed to the eternal truths discovered in 1963, totally impervious to any doubt, anxiety, reconsideration. But there are anxieties of another kind. What if innocent students of history actually begin to consider questions raised by subsequent research both on the perspective as well as on data that constitute the bedrock of Habib's thesis? In a couple of recent essays published in the name of M. Athar Ali (but with a curious stylistic and linguistic affinity with Irfan Habib's) the anxieties have been reflected in asserting that all documented research done subsequently only reaffirms the findings of "the early 1960s" and any deviations constitute merely "the smoke of verbiage easily blown away!" It seems two lessons that Habib did forget to learn from Marx were to doubt everything, including oneself, and to recognise that if society changes, historiography too does not remain stuck in its original grooves. The awe-inspiring historiography that Habib gave us in the 1960s (his last great piece of writing in this reviewer's view was "Potentialities of Capitalistic Development" in 1968) is today a dead history. Dead and deadening. That is what the absence of self-questioning can turn the most stimulating minds into: dead and deadening. What could really be sadder?

Urdu's Tribute to a Great Teacher

The Annual of Urdu Studies # 9, 1994

Christopher Shackle, ed., ***Urdu and Muslim South Asia: Studies in Honour of Ralph Russell,*** **The School of Oriental and African Studies, London, 1989, Indian edition, Delhi: Oxford University Press, 1991, pp. 205.**

This is a festschrift to honour Ralph Russell, one of the most eminent scholars of Urdu language and literature in the Western world. From the glowing tributes several of his students pay him, Russell would appear to have taught literature in Britain with a missionary zeal. For Urdu, to him, was a point of entry into a whole civilisation of South Asia, a civilisation no longer "out there" but which had come home to Britain itself with the substantial presence of South Asians in the old Isles.

The volume covers diverse themes, not all of them related to Urdu or to Muslim South Asia, much less to Urdu *and* Muslim Asia, the editor's brave attempt to bind them in a common thread in his Introduction notwithstanding.

Professor Shackle opens his Introduction with the statement that the apparent exaggeration of claims on behalf of Urdu by its speakers apart, few, however, "would seriously dispute its significance as the major cultural language for the last two centuries of the Muslims of South Asia..." Despite Shackle's certitude, this is one of the most fiercely contestable statements he has made in the volume, at least amongst the speakers of the language in India. But then Shackle is really addressing his audience in Pakistan where the language, "... developed by the Muslims as the medium in which to reformulate their identity as a colonial minority," finally achieved national status. India, where even by Shackle's criterion, more Muslims (and therefore more Urdu-speakers) live than in Pakistan, does not really count for much. There are in addition other non-Muslim speaken of the language whose existence in any case is excluded by Shackle's definition. The identification of Urdu with Muslims is repeated several times in the Introduction ("Since Urdu only emerged as the premier cultural language of the Muslims of South Asia... towards the end of the eighteenth century...", p. 3); the consequential counterposition of the Muslim and, in particular, the Hindu cultural identities is really evocative of a rather dated historical perspective. Indeed, Shackle transfers this perspective even to some other contributions. Thus the Introduction tranforms "the cultural divide between the two communities," at best a sidelight in the articles of Rupert Snell on Raskhan and D.J. Matthews on the *Kulliyāt* of Quli Qutb Shah, into their main focus (pp. 3–4). To be fair to the contributors, very few of them would stand by the editor's assumptions. In its origin Urdu was the lingua franca of the urban literati, just as English is today in South Asia; Urdu was no more the language of Muslims than English is of the Christians in the subcontinent.

The lead article in the anthology is, appropriately, Victor Kiernan's 'Persian Poetry and Its Cosmopolitan Audience.' Kiernan is a wide-ranging intellectual with an old Marxist worldview; he is also the translator of the poetry of such giants as Iqbal and Faiz into English. It is thus fair to expect a stimulating analysis of the meaning of *ghazal* (his main theme) in Persian and Urdu literatures. He does indeed make frequent incursions into Europe, Turkey, Arabia and China and these lend comparative depth to his analysis. But in the end it is the old Marxist worldview, which must ground every manifestation of life's experience in a "material" (not necessarily economic) basis, that comes in the way of a satisfying exploration.

Ghazal (lit. 'talking to a woman') is by its nature the poetry of love. In the hands of the Arab and Persian Sufi poets where the *ghazal* had originated, its mystic content was expressed in the language of love, of romance. The everlasting longing of the Sufi soul for union with God found utterance in the longing of the lover for the beloved; the ecstasy of union expressed itself in a similar orgasmic ecstasy of lovers after a life of waiting and pining; Kiernan's explanation of such poetry:

> Romantic love between man and woman has been an instinct of every human community from the most primitive to the refined.... But everywhere it has been checked and hemmed-in by encroaching regulations and bans, very often following on class division. In many regions, and in Asia at large by contrast with Europe, it came to be particularly outlawed, and could hardly survive except in disguise. One cloak was supplied by the Sufi concept of the divine Lover (p. 14).
>
> There could be no full release, for the less hardened among the dominant classes from the morass of oppression and corruption in which they lived and moved and had their earthly being. Mystic poetry offered a substitute, escape from consciousness of the unpleasant realities, social as well as personal, that must have haunted them (p. 15).
>
> Sufi poetry was in essence the wail of ossified society, a self-imprisoned civilization. The old order could only go on moldering, all the worse attributes of the Asiatic state worsening as it grew more decrepit, until Western intrusion brought about a painful and costly new start (*Ibid*).

This is pure murder—of some of the most subtle and moving poetry in any literature. This is no more than an illustration of Marx's crude dictum on religion: "a mere reflex of the real world", an escape from the "real" life. Quite apart from the fact that romance, love, and sexual pleasure were frowned upon with far greater fury by the medieval and early modern Christian Church in Europe than by Islam (or Hinduism) in this part of the world, the very assumption that life, or the world, is divided into two halves—the "real", i.e., material, and the cultural or religious or poetic that is "unreal" or a mere "cloak" or "escape" from the real world—is highly problematic, to put it mildly. It is not easy to understand how a religious devotee's experience of his devotion is less real, or mere escape, than the experience of making a living, for example, or a Sufi's ecstasy in what he expriences as his union with God any the less real, or a "cloak", a surrogate sexual pleasure because he has been deprived of such pleasure in "real life". It is because Kiernan, following Marx, makes this rather crude division that he disposes of all the subtlety of Sufi poetry, with ill-concealed disdain, as somewhat unbecoming of man who would rather dare to stand up and face the grim realities of life. (Incidentally, Professor Irfan Habib too, in a recent statement, found this poetry "vulgar" owing to its sexual allusions. One is hard put to identify the source of his outburst—is it his "Marxism" or puritanism?)

In the process Kiernan misses the point that creators of the *ghazal* did in fact stand up to the "realities" of life and protest. For the most striking feature of the *ghazal* is the celebration of *gham* (quite untranslatable, but close to the delight of sorrow or pain). To the fanatic ulema, the theologians, who *argued* out their support for conquest, suppression and extermination by the rulers, the Sufis and the *ghazal*-poets counterposed the "reasons of the heart"—love, compassion, devotion. Against the inhuman "sanity" of the world of conquerors and their ideologues, the poets celebrated the humane "insanity" of the lover. Against the craving for "success" by the mighty and the dominant, the poet courted "failure". The eternal longing of the lover for his beloved, implying eternal failure to unite with the beloved, became a value in itself, an end. The beloved could be anyone, anything: God, woman, a cause, humanity, always immensely beautiful and sensual. The unending longing for the "beloved" and the courting of failure were thus constantly counterposed to the search for success at the other end. This demarcation itself was a form of protest, a strong protest. It was not an escape from life, but an encounter head-on, from the opposite end. The ridicule to which the orthodoxy of the ulema, religious rituals, the might of the powerful and, not least, some of the basic tenets of Islam itself are reduced in Persian and Urdu *ghazal* literature makes it essentially a poetry of protest even at the hands of those poets who are not known for protesting.

Historian Peter Hardy's 'The Mughals and Money' is an interesting exercise in that he extends the meaning of "exchange" from its narrowly economic content to a wide range of "exchange" relationships emanating from a hierarchical social order. "Rulers and hierarchs are seen as exchanging freedom from physical labor for legitimacy, craftsmen and merchants an assured supply of skills for an assured supply of raw materials and an assured market for the finished goods" (p. 10), and so on.

However, having outlined this vast perspective, Hardy decided to narrow down his focus to the attitude of medieval India's "opinion leaders" towards money. Despite a somewhat sketchy treatment of this interesting theme—quite obviouly due to limitations of space—Hardy throws up ideas that could be usefully followed up at some length and could perhaps be linked up with other aspects of economic and social history of medieval India, some of which he has himself mentioned in the opening paragraphs. His conclusion could perhaps be summed up in his own words:

> Members of the Persian-knowing elites of Mughal India regard money as a respectable social phenomenon. But it is one respectable phenomenon among several. Money is certainly not seen as expressing the highest values that man should attain and can attain in his membership of human society...(pp. 22–23).

Interesting, if not a surprising conclusion, which, if Hardy were a Marxist, could be plausibly reduced to a further extension: money, and therefore profit, not having attained the central place in men's thinking at the elite levels, any chance of capitalism emerging from that economy was rather remote. Thoughtful as Hardy's article is, its place in the anthology is slightly less than clear.

Rupert Snell's 'Raskhan the Neophyte: Hindu Perspective on a Muslim Vaishnava' is a well-researched and interesting article which sets out with the rather limited objective of identifying the Muslim Pathan devotee of Krishna. In the process Snell abbreviates and fairly interprets two Vaishnavite texts in which Raskhan is mentioned, deriving meanings from them in the context of Hindu perceptions of the Muslims, some charitable, others not quite.

'The *Kulliyāt* of Muhammad Quli Qutb Shah: Problems and Prospects' by D.J. Mathews is a purely technical, though competent, discussion of the problems of identifying and editing the text of the *Kulliyāt* (complete collection of verses).

Simon Digby's 'An Eighteenth Century Narrative of a Journey from Bengal to England: Munshi Ismāils' *New History*' is a readable anecdotal account. It is difficult to see what else it is. It has nothing to do with Muslims except that the author of the travelogue was a Muslim. Digby does seek to establish its linkage with South Asian Muslims by making the somewhat dubious assertion that the Munshi was able to travel all the way to England because he was Muslim, for the Hindus were deterred by their caste rules from crossing the "Black Water" (p. 51). Rather than taking the caste injuction as evidence of the ground reality, a historian, one thought, was expected to compare the injunction with the ground reality. Digby also constructs queer phrases in English such as "geographical knowledge of Europe"(p. 49) when he means "Europeans' knowledge of geography".

'Emperor of India: Landhaur bin Sadān in the *Hamza* Cycle' by Frances W. Pritchett examines the Urdu version of the *dāstān* (prose romance) tradition of Persian literature. For her study Pritchett takes up perhaps the best known work in this tradition in the Persian language, the *Qiṣṣa-e Ḥamza* and looks at its "most popular Urdu version" Abdullah Bilgrami's *Dāstān-e Ḥamza*, first published in Lucknow in 1871.

What is fascinating about the Urdu *dāstān* is that in its transition from Persian to Urdu the story acquires such thoroughly Indian characteristic as would have been unthinkable in the original version, a point stirikingly brought out by Pritchett. In Persian, Landhaur is the son of the king Sarandib, vaguely identified with Sri Lanka; Landhaur is also a rather marginal character. But in the Urdu version he become the "Emperor of India" and occupies centre stage. The name Landhaur also ges identified in several 19th-century Urdu dictionaries with the mythical Karna of the Mahābhārata. Several of the incidents in the Urdu *dāstān* are its own creations.

> Landhaur's career as an Indian dastan hero is thus a spectacular one. He grows from being one vague king among many—as he was born in Iran—into a figure of unique vividness, power, nobility, and intimacy with Hamzah. Landhaur rides an Indian elephant, commands an Indian army, and has an Indian history. If Hamza is one half of a South Asian Muslim's heritage, Landhaur is the other (p. 72).

Christopher Shackle's fascinating paper, 'Urdu as a Sideline: The Poetry of Khwāja Ghulām Farid,' compares the 19th-century Sufi poet's compositions in Urdu and his mother-tongue Siraiki. Quite persuasively Shackle dismisses his Urdu poetry as considerably inferior in literary quality to the other, the Khwaja's boasts notwithstanding. Shackle's mastery of both the Urdu and Siraiki languages is established by his excellent translation of verses, though just for once I would have preferred *vaḥshat* being rendered as passion rather than insanity (p. 85). But beyond the words, metaphors and similes employed by Khwaja Farid, the basic tenets of both the Sufi life-experience and the *ghazal* form come through so very strikingly in his verses: love, devotion, liberal humanism and defiance of religious orthodoxy. To cite just a couple of verses:

> To me the Kaaba now an idol-temple seems
> And this is my cry of faith a Christian church's bell
> (p.82)
>
> These idols' tresses hold my heart, so I
> Shun faith as others do impiety (*kufr*)
> (p. 85)

It is only the Sufi-*ghazal* form that could suspect an idol-temple beneath the holy of holies of Islam, the Kaaba itself (compare also Ghalib); and the Kafir, the one most virulently despised by ulema, acquires the meaning of the longed-for sweetheart in the *ghazal* (compare Ghalib again).

Barbara D. Metcalf's 'Maulāna Ashraf Ali Thānavī and Urdu Literature' and Gail Minault's '*Ismat*: Rashid ul-Khairi's Nobels and Urdu Literary Journalism for Women' are both interesting explorations in Muslim men's attempts to introduce mild social reform for their women through the promotion of elementary education and literacy among them. Minault brings out particularly poignantly both the sensitivity of such men to women as individuals and their readiness to draw back in horror when the endeavours initiated by them seem to cross the threshold they had set. Both the studies are situated in the fast-changing scenario of the late 19th and early 20th centuries.

Francis Robinson in his '*An-Nizāmiyya*: A Group of Lucknow Intellectuals in the Early Twentieth Century' forcefully traces the attempt by an eminent family of Lucknow intellectuals, located in Farangi Mahal, to re-establish Islamic solidarity at elite levels within their community by running schools and establishing a journal, *An -Nizāmiyya*. Robinson situates this attempt in the rapidly changing context of the period, but alas, this context remains a somewhat distant shadow, for space does not permit him to deal with the surrounding circumstances in any detail.

Christian W. Troll translates an essay on 'Sarmad the Martyr' by Maulāma Abul Kalam Āzād to make just one important point—that the Maulana's commitment to composite nationalism derived from his Sufic inclinations and that this commitment preceded his involvement with parties and their politics. Troll makes the point well; his translation also retain the flavour of the Maulana's distinctive idiom.

Muhammad Umar Memon analyses one novel in 'Shi'ite Consciousness in a Recent Urdu Novel: Intrizār Husain's

Basti.' The story is placed in post-1971 Pakistan when anger moved the country's youth following its disintegration. But the novel's hero, young Zakir, suffers instead of rebelling, remains detached rather than raising his hands in indignation. Husain had been criticized by other reviewers for turning his hero into a 'coward.' Memon contextualizes the 'cowardice' and particularly the suffering of Zakir in his Shiite consciousness and very powerfully brings out the force of suffering as a "mode of resistance, of denial, of disapproval"(p. 149). Memon's is excellent literary criticism and superb contextualisation; the entire anthology is worth the while for this one essay.

Khalid Hasan Qadiri gives details of the art of the chronogram as practised by his father, Maulana Hamid Hasan Qadiri.

Each letter in the Arabic script carries a numerical value and therefore a certain combination of letters in a phrase or a verse would add up to a given total which is used to indicate the year of the occurrence of an event. This is the chronogram. Historically the art was useful for ensuring the precise chronological location of events; today it is an archaic art, charming like an old relic whose charm is not to be valued in terms of utility. Qadiri goes into various technicalities of such compositions; he knows the craft well.

C.M. Naim prepares a purely "introductory" kind of note for familiarizing the unfamiliar with what a 'mushaira' is and how it is conducted. His paper is titled 'Poet-Audience Interaction at Urdu Mushairas.'

Regula Bruckhardt Qureshi too introduces the musical element of the Urdu *ghazal* as it is sung; she clearly has the Western audience in view.

Finally, Marion Molteno recalls and compliments Ralph Russell's vision and effort on behalf of Urdu in Britain in " 'This New Work': Ralph Russell and Urdu in Britain". The volume concludes with a select bibliography of Russell's works.

The essays in the anthology run to fairly uniform length;

clearly, the editor was able to enforce his instructions to the contribution on this score fairly rigorously. Which, I think, is a mixed blessing, for some of the papers did require a bit more elbow room to make their points effectively. At any rate, and irrespective of that, barring a couple of papers, I am not sure whether the anthology as a whole advances our understanding of either Urdu or Muslim South Asia in any significant way.

Islam in India

Richard M. Eaton (ed.), ***India's Islamic Traditions, 711–1750,*** **Oxford University Press, New Delhi, 2003, (Series: Themes in Indian History), pp. 439.**

Muhammad Ashraf Wani, ***Islam in Kashmir (Fourteenth to Sixteenth Century),*** **Oriental Publishing House, Srinagar, 2004, pp. xiii + 338.**

Richard Eaton's major presence in the writing of medieval Indian history is guarantee enough of the high quality of work he undertakes, as he has done in this volume. It comprises 17 well-known essays and a long, scholarly Introduction. The volume is divided into five parts: representing Self and Other; religion and political power; history, literature and law; Sufi and Shi'i traditions; and Islam in the regions of India.

If there is one binding thread that runs through most of the anthology, it is the multisided nature of India's Islamic traditions, or the 'fluidity of Indo-Islamic identities' (p. 27), in Eaton's words. The Introduction highlights two aspects of the endeavour: the historigraphical shifts that have occurred since the 1960s and the multi-dimensionality of the shift from the simple binary to the complex interactive. One would have little to quarrel with the argument except on one not-so-small a point: when Eaton builds a thesis on the basis of the use of the ethnic term 'Turk' in lieu of the religious denominational term 'Muslim' in medieval India's 'Hindu' sources, he assumes a conscious differentiation between the two and a considered preference for one over the other. By itself it is not a new argument, but new or old, it does seem anachronistically to transfer a much later strategy of establishing the difference into the medieval centuries. For much of our evidence, including that of Eleanor Zelliot's essay in the volume, does seem to suggest equivalence rather than differentiation between 'Turk' and 'Muslim' in medieval consciousness. But the Introduction is nevertheless a treat.

The first essay of Aziz Ahmad, from the 1963 vintage, captures that binary category of Hindu/Muslim in the two geners of epics— 'the Muslim epic of conquest and the Hindu epic of resistance' (p. 37)— composed in medieval India. It therefore makes a good starting point for the book to trace the layout of the shifts in history-writing since, although the dividing lines are chronologically anything but firm. To a large extent, the same thread runs through the next essay of Yohann Friedmann, 'Islamic Thought in Relation to the Indian Context' (1986). His argument is best summed up in his own formulation: The conciliatory trend [in Indian Islam] was always weaker than the orthodox one. If Dara Shukoh encapsulated the 'conciliatory trend' his execution in 1659 symbolically sealed its fate too.

The other essays in the volume question precisely these neat dichotomies of Hindu/Muslim, liberal/orthodox. Eleanor Zelliot's English rendering of the 16th century Maharashtrian saint-poet Eknath's *Hindu–Turk Samvad* (1982) demonstrates the flimsiness of the dichotomy even as it recognises the existence of the distinctive identities of the two and even as it hits hard at the stridency of both. In a way Cynthia Talbot views the same problem in a different regional as well as textual context 'Inscribing the Other, Inscribing the Self: Hindu–Muslim Identities in Pre-colonial India' (1995). She explores 'the history of the mutual- and self-perception' of the two recovered from a hundred records in Sanskrit and Telugu languages in medieval Andhra region. As most of the inscriptions are located in Hindu temple complexes, the religious idiom becomes integral to them, at times in harsh expressions. The inscriptions speak of atrocities of the Muslims on the Hindus as the Muslim arms advanced into the Deccan territories; they also evoke images of a varied and varying relationship between Muslim rulers and Hindu subjects. Yet, some features emerge in salience: all temple desecration occurred in contested territory, and there is no case of this nature within the land ruled by Muslims. This point has indeed been made earlier in other contexts by several historians; that, however, in no way diminishes the significance of the conclusions drawn by Talbot from a careful study of the large number of inscriptions spread over a long stretch of time.

Part 2 opens with Iqtidar Alam Khan's classic essay, 'The Nobility Under Akbar and the Development of His Religious Policy, 1560–80', first published in 1968. A couple of years before the essay was published and when its argument was presumably evolving in the author's mind, M. Athar Ali's *Mughal Nobility Under Aurangzeb* had made its appearance (1966, Bombay). Both these studies altered the parameters of the problematic of what was then known as 'the religious policy of the Mughals'. Contrary to the 'religious policy' motif, which perceived the 'policy' entirely as the unfolding of personal beliefs and religious predilections of the emperors, Athar Ali and Iqtidar Alam Khan embedded the policy in the political context. One major consequence was to visualise 'religious policy' not as an unvarying manifestation of the predisposition of the ruler, but as a constantly shifting stance catering to the changing requirements of the state's imperatives. Khan's article did not go unquestioned, though. Some of the empirical bases of his argument, especially the issuing of the highly religiously charged *fathnama* ('proclamation of victory') after Akbar's defeat of the 'infidel' Rana Pratap, have been found to be less than solid; but the big picture stands and alters the historiographical landscape. Following in the footsteps of Athar Ali and I.A. Khan, Satish Chandra too endeavoured in 1969 to reformulate Aurangzeb's 'religious policy' by placing his re-imposition of the *jizia* in a political context. That is the next essay.

Derryl N. MacLean (2000) reopens the problem of relationship between the Mahdawi movement in India and the Afghan and the Mughal states from the middle of the 16th to the late 17th century. The movement had chiefly been launched by the enviably learned and impeccably honest Sayyid Muhammad of Jaunpur and had been perceived then as now in essentially adversarial terms by historians. MacLean nuances the perception by dividing it up into phases, the early one marked by opposition and the later by 'compromise' and 'political disengagement'—a very valuable revision.

Part 3 opens with Peter Hardy's 1960 essay, part of his doctoral thesis, on some general characteristics of history writing during the Delhi Sultanate period. His *Historians of Medieval India* (1960, London) was a pioneering effort in the area and thus had all the energy and the flaws of such an endeavour. If it opened up a new problematic and inspired several subsequent works in this genre, its chief problem was that it took the historians he was analysing far too much on their stated word, even when they were crying out for being read between the lines. His general thesis that history for medieval historians was a branch of theology fits in far more cosily with the European than the Indian context.

From court history, we move to the genre of folk epic with Aditya Behl's essay on 'Desire and Narrative in a Hindavi Sufi Romance', where he analyses the early 16th century romance, *Mrgavati*, by Qutban. Behl takes us through a very subtle and multisided tour through intertwining bylanes of history, economy, religion and literature to make the valuable point that even as medieval India's Sufi litterateurs were creating a separate Muslim literary identity, the sources and the idioms were drawn from the entire Indian Ocean region, including its diverse religions. It thus becomes a deeply cultural rather than religious exercise, "where societies of the period are best understood as linked families of cultural practice" (p.205). The essay is part of Behl's forthcoming work *Shadows of Paradise: and Indian Literary Tradition, 1379–1545*. A work surely worth waiting for.

Alan M. Guenther's study of the *Fatawa-i Alamgiri* is very detailed examination of the technical aspects of the work and of *fatawa* in general and yields important information. It does not purport to be an analysis. It probably makes its first appearance in this volume.

Part 4 brings us to the 1986 essay of Simon Digby on 'The Sufi Shaikh as a Source of Authority in Medieval India'. Digby too, like the late Professor K.A. Nizami has studied Indian Sufis and Sufism for a lifetime. If Nizami was a trifle too deferential to the subjects of his study, Digby stands at the other end, looking at the Sufis in very human terms, as persons with large egos and small hearts as much as people with a grand vision and quality of leadership, which gave them a source of authority that many of the sultans envied. Digby's is forever a historian's quest, inquisitive and irreverent, of which this essay is an excellent example. This is followed by Richard Eaton's own contribution, drawn from a 1984 volume, on 'The Political and Religious Authority of Baba Farid'. As a theme it parallels (even as it precedes) Digby's; but the treatment is vastly diferent. In many ways it presages Eaton's magnificent work on *The Rise of Islam and the Bengal Frontier*, which was to appear a decade later. It looks at the problem from a range of angles: sociology, economy, ecology, hagiography, state...

Ali S. Asnani next gives us a synoptic introduction (1996) to the Khojah Ismailis of South Asia (mainly Gujarat), a group that stands at the intersection of the Sunni and Shi'i Muslims and the Hindus. He takes us through the details of the ceremonies, rituals, beliefs and above all their sacred songs, the *ginans*. J.R.I. Cole (1988) in turn, lays out a broad picture of popular Shi'ism in Awadh in the 18th and 19th centuries. Although, as the author observes at the outset, the Shi'i practice of cursing the caliphs honoured by Sunnis and forbidding Hindu celebrations during Muharram mourning encouraged the growth of incipient communalism, he traces out the outreaches of Awadh culture that spread out and took in Hindus and Sunni Muslims into its fold and which also put it beyond the Shi'i confines.

The last part has at its head M. Ishaq Khan's exploration of the specific Kashmiri character of Islam in the region whose transition to the new religion was mediated through the Rishi tradition. Thus, far from Hinduism and Islam being constituted in oppositional terms, the blending between the two here was almost unselfconscious and therefore durable. Khan had experimented with this research strategy in 1986 in the article reproduced here; he followed it up with a full length study in 1994. It is only now that an alternative view has been propounded by Khan's colleague in the next book reviewed here.

Tony K. Stewart seeks to create a largely theoretical apparatus to explore what he calls the 'Muslim–Hindu Encounter' through translation theory (2001). Translation here is not the formal exercise but the transmission, refraction, appropriation of the idiom of one religion into another. The last contribution, first published in 2000, is from Vasudha Narayanan in a way pursuing the same theme of 'translation' at an empirical level by looking at the medieval Tamil work *Cirappuranam* (Life of the Prophet of Islam). The author of the biography was Umaru Pulavar (Umar the poet) who died in 1703. Considering that Tamil Muslims claim to have converted to Islam during the lifetime of Muhammad himself and were thus the earliest to have converted, the biography is a very late work, even as it is the most famous. The conclusion is far from surprising to the professional historian, though Narayanan adds weight to it:' ... by using established tropes of classical literature, Umaru manages to incorporate the Prophet into a Tamil world that is shared by both Muslims and Hindus' (p. 403). Indeed the title of the work itself is a compound of two words: Arabic—*sira* (essence or life) and Sanskrit/Tamil—*puranam* (old anecdotes).

Richard Eaton has been discriminating in identifying

essays for this excellent volume; the result matches with his effort.

Muhammad Ashraf Wani's *Islam in Kashmir* expands the space mapped by its predecessor, M. Ishaq Khan's *Kashmir's Transition to Islam* published a decade ago. Whereas Ishaq Khan had attributed the 'transition' almost exclusively to Kashmir's *rishi* tradition which had its origins in Hinduism but which was also organised into a Muslim *silsilah* by Shaikh Nur al- din Rishi, Ashraf Wani, even while giving the due to the *rishi*, explores several other inputs into the process. Besides the archives and texts, he also undertakes fieldwork to analyse the transfer of surnames with or without change of religion, folk sayings and archaeological data—all of these innovatively and effectively. As a welcome departure, Wani also delves deep into Sanskrit sources to understand the pre-Islamic social and cultural morés in the region.

Ashraf Wani then puts forward his argument that besides the efforts of Shaikh Nur al-Din, Kashmir turned to Islam on account of the endeavours of Sayyid Ali Hamdani, the Central Asian missionary, who turned his attention to the rulers and nobles rather than to the mass of Kashmiris on the assumption that common people will emulate the lifestyles of the elite. Thus, even as the state used no force in the process of conversion, it set an example which was followed by the subjects. Ashraf Wani lays considerabvle emphasis on this factor and does not seem to accept that the common people too have a mind of their own and their 'emulation' of the elites, wherever it occurs, happens for reasons other than their lack of intelligence or education or culture.

In analysing the reasons for mass conversion to Islam, Ashraf Wani seeks to contrast the moral degeneration of the Hindus, following the prevalence of Shavite *tantrik* practices, manifest in sexual licentiousness and conssumption of liquor, and the puritanical life of the Sufi preachers which registered an appeal with the masses. Thus coversion in Kashmir was a 'genuine turnover of public opinion' (p.149), he asserts invoking a phrase Muhammad Habib had used over a half century ago in the context of Ghurids in north India. Besides, the Muslims from Central Asia and Iran brought new technology with them and this brought economic prosperity and conversions. To these he adds several other factors like the performance of miracles by the Sufis, the class oppression of the Damaras over the mass of people and religious discord amont the Hindus.

It would be hard for Ashraf Wani to expect that his propositions could go uncontested among historians. Still, it is important that he has sought out new dimensions, used new sources and asked some new questions, even as he reaffirms the old assertion that the use of state force has no role in the Kashmir valley going the Islam way on such a massive scale.